Teaching Math to Students with Learning Disabilities
Implications and Solutions

**John F. Cawley, Anne Hayes,
and Teresa E. Foley**

Published in Partnership with
Learning Disabilities Worldwide

Rowman & Littlefield Education
Lanham • New York • Toronto • Plymouth, UK

Published in Partnership with
Learning Disabilities Worldwide

Published in the United States of America
by Rowman & Littlefield Education
A Division of Rowman & Littlefield Publishers, Inc.
A wholly owned subsidary of The Rowman & Littlefield Publishing Group, Inc.
4501 Forbes Boulevard, Suite 200, Lanham, Maryland 20706
www.rowmaneducation.com

Estover Road
Plymouth PL6 7PY
United Kingdom

British Library Cataloguing in Publication Information Available

Library of Congress Cataloging-in-Publication Data

Cawley, John F.
    Teaching math to students with learning disabilities : implications and solutions / John F. Cawley, Anne Hayes, and Teresa E. Foley.
        p. cm.
    Includes bibliographical references.
    ISBN-13: 978-1-57886-824-7 (cloth : alk. paper)
    ISBN-10: 1-57886-824-6 (cloth : alk. paper)
    ISBN-13: 978-1-57886-825-4 (pbk. : alk. paper)
    ISBN-10: 1-57886-825-4 (pbk. : alk. paper)
    eISBN-13: 978-1-57886-893-3
    eISBN-10: 1-57886-893-9
    1. Mathematics—Study and teaching. 2. Problem solving—Study and teaching.
3. Arithmetic—Study and teaching. 4. Learning disabled children—Education—
Mathematics. I. Hayes, Anne, 1941– II. Foley, Teresa E., 1964– III. Title.
QA11.2C39 2008
371.9'0447—dc22   2008011222

♾™ The paper used in this publication meets the minimum requirements of
American National Standard for Information Sciences—Permanence of
Paper for Printed Library Materials, ANSI/NISO Z39.48-1992.
Manufactured in the United States of America.

This book is dedicated to Louise J. Cawley, companion, advisor, and advocate, whose many years of cooperation and assistance with our many projects is deeply appreciated.

Contents

Introduction   vii

CHAPTER 1: Problem Solving Precedes Computation   1

CHAPTER 2: Developing Word Problems for Diagnostic Feedback   29

CHAPTER 3: Connections to Other Subjects   43

CHAPTER 4: Arithmetic Computation   61

CHAPTER 5: Knowing about and Being Able to Do   73

CHAPTER 6: Communicating Mathematics   91

CHAPTER 7: Teaching the Operations Using Whole Numbers   109

CHAPTER 8: Hand-Held Calculators   143

CHAPTER 9: Concluding Comments   149

APPENDIX: Computational Sequences   151

References   157

About the Authors   161

Introduction

Purposes of Mathematics

The focus of this book is the arithmetic of whole numbers for students who have difficulties in mathematics. In this regard, we envision two primary purposes for the mathematics. The first purpose is that programs assure students *a wide range of opportunities to know about the many meanings and principles of mathematics* and to *develop proficiency with a variety of ways of doing and representing mathematics.* The second purpose is that the programs utilize *mathematics activities to enhance students' performance in areas such as language comprehension, social-personal development, cognitive growth, and all the other limitations ascribed to students with difficulties in mathematics.* In this regard, it is our intent to demonstrate how the activities of mathematics can be utilized to ameliorate limitations or disabilities that are often given as the reason why students have difficulties in mathematics.

This book is directed toward qualitative outcomes in programming and their implications for students with difficulties in mathematics in both regular and special education programs. The book is intended to offer alternatives to the traditional rote and passive learning that characterizes much of the mathematics education of children with difficulties in mathematics. This is not a methods text, nor is it a curriculum text. Rather, in a manner consistent with both the National Council of Teachers of Mathematics and the goals of special education established by the Council of Exceptional Children, it is a framework. Consequently, we provide illustrations and examples of what ought to be done and what can be done, most of which are based on our own work and that of others who work with mathematics and students with difficulties in mathematics. Ultimately, what is done in the classroom is a local matter for the district and teacher.

Qualitative outcomes focus on the acquisition of factual knowledge and the meanings and principles that integrate various forms of factual knowledge. Having factual knowledge is distinguished from knowing facts. Qualitative outcomes result from instructional practices that are meaningful in form and that involve the students in authentic or situated learning experiences, or experiences that are contrived in such a way that they interest or challenge the students. Qualitative outcomes are evident when the students can explain, demonstrate, prove and elaborate on alternative "ways of doing and knowing" and when the students express satisfaction with what is known and how it gives meaning to self and life.

Perspective

The perspective from which this book is written is rooted in the work of one of the foremost pioneers in the field of special education, Edward Seguin, who in 1866 wrote:

We must never confide to automatic memory what can be learned by comparison, nor teach a thing without its natural correlations and generalizations; otherwise, we give a false or incomplete idea, or none, but a dry notion with a name; what enters the mind alone, dies in it alone; loneliness does not germinate anything. The contact of two perceptions produce an idea; the contact of a perception with an idea produces a deductive idea; the contact of two or more ideas with each other gives rise to both induction and deduction and ideas of an abstract order (Seguin, 1866, p. 67).

Within the context of P.L. 94-142, The Education of All Handicapped Children's Act, it is clear that special education is to be provided to children who *require* special education to meet their *unique* needs. It is also clear, in both The Education of All Handicapped Children's Act (EHA) and P.L. 105-17, The Individuals with Disabilities Education Act (IDEA), that children with disabilities are to be educated to the maximum extent possible with students who do not have disabilities. The amendments to IDEA (Federal Register, 1999) extend the latter to stress access and progress in the general education curriculum. Further, these amendments define the general education curriculum as essentially the same curriculum as presented to students who do not have disabilities. The combination of general education experiences for students with disabilities and the stipulation that the general education curriculum is essentially that which is provided to students who do not have disabilities has ominous implications for both special educators and mathematics educators.

The What and When of Mathematics Programming

We envision curriculum or content as both the *what* and *when* of the educational offerings that will be presented to the students. Decisions as to *what* will be presented to the students comprise the most important decision by school personnel. Decisions as to *when* various meanings, skills, and processes will be offered to the individual guide us in the organization of curriculum content. Does this suggest, for example, that students with difficulties in mathematics who are achieving three or more years below their grade level will receive the general education curriculum for their present level of functioning or for their existing age levels? Curriculum decisions also involve *sequence* relative to prerequisites and prior knowledge; *intensity*, or whether one adopts a spiral or intensified system of organization; and *range*, or whether one presents a diverse or limited amount of knowledge, processes, and skills. With respect to sequence, the traditional sequence for the operations on whole numbers is addition, subtraction, multiplication, and division. This sequence, while common and generally effective, is not absolutely necessary. For example, as we will show, one can teach division before subtraction or multiplication. To do so, one only needs to use an algorithm that does not require subtraction or multiplication.

Instructional methods, or the *how* of the educational program, are an integral aspect of specially designed programming. Instructional decisions are important because they assist in guaranteeing the student access to the processes and content that comprise the program. For example, assume a decision was made to teach a unit on arithmetic problem solving. The curriculum, or content, decision has been made. Assume that the classroom consists of both students with disabilities in mathematics and students who do not have disabilities in mathematics. Also assume that the traditional means for teaching a topic such as arithmetic problem solving involves reading from a text. Yet, one of the limitations frequently associated with students having difficulties in mathematics is that they may have difficulties in reading (Fuchs & Fuchs, 2002). Alternative instructional methods must be utilized, especially an approach that minimizes reading. Instruction is also influenced by the *rate of presentation*; *mass*, or how much will be covered in given periods of time; *empowerment*, or the amount of responsibility that will be given to the students; and *activation*, or the degree to which the students will be held accountable for activating strategies and other mechanisms to monitor and guide individual and group learning. Differences in the *how* might be illustrated by the extent to which the teachers direct and monitor students' performance in some form of rate-in-time format (e.g., students are to complete work in a given period of time) or in some form of problem-solving format (e.g., the teacher involves students in activities and provides ample opportunity for them to complete the activities). The former views the teacher as "nudging" and reinforcing the students to work actively. The latter views the teacher in a "wait time" mode where the students are encouraged to ponder.

A Primary Purpose

A primary purpose of this book devoted to whole numbers is to describe ways and means by which the limitations attributed to the students can be bypassed or circumvented so that students' achievement will be characterized by high levels of outcomes and students demonstrate that they know a great deal about mathematics and that they can do a variety of mathematics in a variety of ways. What we will do in this book is describe ways in which mathematics can be taught independent of limitations in reading and other developmental characteristics and, in fact, show how mathematics activities can be used to generate competence in these processes, even with topics such as arithmetic problem solving. Within the realm of mathematics itself, we will illustrate procedures whereby a limitation in arithmetical competence can be bypassed so the students can attain mastery with the desired outcome. For example, a study by Bryant, Bryant, and Hammill (2000) showed that teachers perceive limitations in "borrowing/renaming" as a major difficulty in subtraction among students with mathematical difficulties. We will demonstrate that subtraction can be taught without "borrowing/renaming," that is, the students can first be taught to do subtraction without "borrowing/renaming" and subsequently be introduced to the traditional algorithm. In effect, we will demonstrate that it is possible to adapt the mathematics to address the needs of the students in contrast to the customary approach, which seeks to challenge the students to do mathematics solely in the traditional manner.

With respect to problem solving, the great majority of problem solving in school programs focuses on the traditional format that provides three or four information statements followed by a question that linguistically cues the students to the operation to be performed (Foley, Parmar, & Cawley, 2003, 2004; Fuchs & Fuchs, 2002). From our early work (Cawley & Goodman, 1969) through our current efforts (Foley, Parmar, & Cawley, 2003, 2004), we have taken the position that the traditional format of word problems is inadequate and fails to offer a system that will develop competence with word problems of varying structures. Further, we have supported an approach that demands more of the students than simply the correct answer. In this regard, we encourage teachers to have students (a) explain and describe similarities and differences in word problems of varying types, (b) prove the relationship between the information set (i.e., the three or four sentences of the problem) and the steps to solution, (c) create word problems of varying structures and explain what they did to make one problem similar to or different from another, and (d) participate in long-term problem-solving activities lasting a few weeks to a year. What we seek to accomplish is higher levels of outcomes for students with mathematical difficulties and in so doing, provide the students with a sense of self-worth by stressing the importance of knowing a variety of principles and meanings and by developing proficiency with a variety of ways of doing mathematics.

The reader will note that our view of students with difficulties in mathematics is that they are capable of acquiring and demonstrating much higher levels of outcomes in mathematics than has traditionally been shown. They can learn a great deal about mathematics and a great many ways of doing mathematics. They can demonstrate their knowledge and proficiency by (a) explaining and justifying various principles and algorithms, (b) solving and creating problems of varying structures, (c) utilizing a variety of alternative representations of mathematics meanings and routines, and (d) performing to a satisfactory level on assessments of higher-order outcomes.

A Basic Understanding for Teachers

Fundamental to programming and the search for higher-order outcomes for students with difficulties in mathematics is the importance for teachers to understand the principle of *present level of functioning* (PLF). A student's present level of functioning is the level at which the available assessment data and the daily work of the student confirm that the student can perform at a high level of consistency and percent correct. Unfortunately, in most instances, the two data sets seldom distinguish between what a student knows about a given topic and precisely what the student can do in that topic. For example, the typical database may state that the student is fourteen years old and has a test score equivalent to the second grade. The assumption is that the student knows and can do all the things a high-performing second-grade student can do. This is generally a false assumption. The assessment data fail to inform the teacher of the specific types and levels of performance and to link this to an overall pattern of present level of functioning. Further, the assessment data generally fail to inform the teacher of the various ways the teacher might engage the student in representing his or her knowledge about a topic and the extent to which the student can use different algorithms to confirm his or her status.

The daily work of the student is an important indicator of present level of functioning, as it informs the teacher of the extent to which the performance of the student is satisfactory. In a sense, the database that determines the present level of functioning is a high level of percent correct. This requires that the teacher provide lessons on which the student can attain high levels of correct responses day after day or that the student can explain and give a rationale for various principles or meanings. This could be accomplished by a teacher who sets a level of performance for a student at a level of 80 percent correct on each and every task. For example, as a measure of *doing* computation, the teacher might provide the students with the following item and ask them to compute the item and provide a correct response.

$$
\begin{array}{r}
325 \\
+\,324 \\
\end{array}
$$

To assess *knowing*, the teacher might provide the same item in an alternative manner and ask the students to compute the item many different ways by following rules provided as illustrated below.

$$
\begin{array}{r}
A\ B\ C \\
3\ 2\ 5 \\
+\,3\ 2\ 4 \\
\end{array}
$$

Rule 1: Begin with A, add C, then add B.
Rule 2: Begin with B, add C, then add A.

The student who knows about addition knows there are many ways of doing arithmetic, understands the role of place value in the process, is able to relate this to many ways of doing addition, and can complete the item as instructed.

In this book we describe a procedure to organize problem solving by the development of matrices that categorize the problems and denote specifically to the teacher what types of problems the students show satisfactory performance on and what types of problems present difficulties for the students. By examining problem type by level of accuracy within a matrix, the teacher is able to select subsequent lessons and experiences. A similar approach can be undertaken with computation. This approach necessitates the organization of a curriculum sequence in which item choices can be made. Note that we have used the term *item* to designate a computational item when the students are only going to compute. We will designate the item as a problem when we do a problem-solving activity—that is, when we ask the students to reason and prove selected features of their knowledge about an item, represent their solution in a variety of ways, or use and adapt alternative algorithms to solve an item.

Again, our view is that students who experience difficulties in mathematics are capable of acquiring and demonstrating much higher levels of outcomes in mathematics than has traditionally been shown. Thus, it is essential that we think qualitatively and capably about students with difficulties in mathematics. The difficulties might not always be with the students; the difficulties might be in the mathematics, the manner in which they are presented, and the content choices that are made about the mathematics.

## CHAPTER ONE

Problem Solving Precedes Computation

Over the course of many years, arithmetic programming has stressed computation routines in preference to meanings and problem solving. The more appropriate emphasis is a stress on problem solving as the true priority, with the result that problem-solving activities provide meanings and applications for the processes and concepts of the operations. This supports the idea that the reason we learn computation is to provide a database that yields a solution or an alternative to a problem.

The data in the following table illustrate the performance characteristics of students with and without learning disabilities.

Means and Standard Deviations for Verbal Problem-Solving Scores

Problem Type	Grade Group	3 GES	3 SWD	4 GES	4 SWD	5 GES	5 SWD	6 GES	6 SWD	7 GES	7 SWD	8 GES	8 SWD	
Pictures	N	123	26	132	35	130	38	114	39	129	39	109	20	
Basic (6)	Mean	5.2	4.8	5.4	5.1	5.7	5.2	5.7	5.6	5.7	5.3	5.8	5.8	
	SD	1.4	1.6	1.4	0.9	0.8	1.2	0.7	0.6	0.7	1.4	0.5	0.4	
Addition (5)	N	123	26	132	35	130	38	114	39	129	39	109	20	
	Mean	4.2	3.8	4.3	4.1	4.7	4.4	4.7	4.6	4.7	4.4	4.8	4.6	
	SD	1.4	1.8	1.3	1.2	0.8	1.2	0.8	0.7	0.8	1.2	0.5	0.6	
Subtraction	N	123	26	132	35	30	38	114	39	129	39	109	20	
(5)	Mean	2.9	2.5	3.2	2.9	3.5	2.9	3.7	3.3	3.7	3.2	3.3	3.2	
	SD	1.1	0.9	1.1	0.7	0.8	1.0	0.7	0.8	0.6	1.0	0.5	0.8	
Multiplication	N	105	18	116	27	126	32	110	37	125	35	109	20	
(5)	Mean	1.8	1.3	2.7	1.5	3.1	2.2	3.8	2.2	3.8	2.2	3.9	2.1	
	SD	1.5	1.1	1.7	1.2	1.7	1.5	1.5	1.6	1.4	1.4	1.4	1.7	
Division (5)	N	105	18	116	27	126	32	110	37	125	35	109	20	
	Mean	2.7	2.7	3.0	2.3	3.6	2.8	3.8	3.1	4.0	2.8	3.8	2.8	
	SD	1.2	1.2	1.4	1.3	1.2	1.3	1.3	1.1	1.1	1.3	1.2	1.2	
Text Form	N	123	26	132	35	130	38	114	39	29	39	109	20	
Direct	Mean	4.6	2.9	5.1	3.9	5.7	4.1	6.1	4.7	6.4	4.3	6.5	4.6	
Addition/	SD	2.4	1.7	2.4	2.2	2.1	2.4	2.1	2.0	1.9	2.2	1.8	2.2	
Subtraction (8)														

(Continued)

Means and Standard Deviations for Verbal Problem-Solving Scores (Continued)

Problem Type	Grade Group	3 GES	3 SWD	4 GES	4 SWD	5 GES	5 SWD	6 GES	6 SWD	7 GES	7 SWD	8 GES	8 SWD
Direct	N	50	—	72	—	81	13	87	15	99	14	82	—
Multiplication/	Mean	3.6	—	4.5	—	5.4	2.8	5.8	4.3	6.3	3.0	6.3	—
Division (8)	SD	2.2	—	2.4	—	2.2	2.1	2.0	2.0	2.1	2.4	1.8	—
Indirect All (8)	N	10	—	33	—	45	—	55	—	74	—	61	—
	Mean	4.6	—	5.7	—	6.3	—	6.5	—	6.7	—	7.0	—
	SD	2.8	—	1.7	—	1.4	—	1.7	—	1.4	—	1.2	—
Two-Step (8)	N	10	—	33	—	45	—	55	—	74	—	61	—
	Mean	3.5	—	3.8	—	4.2	—	4.6	—	4.6	—	4.7	—
	SD	2.2	—	1.9	—	1.7	—	1.6	—	1.5	—	1.6	—
Decimal (8)	N	—	—	16	—	29	—	38	—	49	—	45	—
	Mean	—	—	5.4	—	6.2	—	6.1	—	6.8	—	6.6	—
	SD	—	—	2.1	—	1.7	—	2.3	—	1.7	—	2.1	—
Fraction (8)	N	—	—	16	—	29	—	38	—	49	—	45	—
	Mean	—	—	1.0	—	3.4	—	3.0	—	4.9	—	4.7	—
	SD	—	—	1.2	—	2.4	—	2.5	—	2.7	—	2.6	—
Percent (8)	N	—	—	16	—	29	—	38	—	49	—	45	—
	Mean	—	—	0.3	—	0.7	—	1.9	—	3.3	—	3.5	—
	SD	—	—	1.0	—	1.2	—	2.5	—	3.0	—	2.9	—
Pre-algebra (6)	N	—	—	16	—	29	—	38	—	49	—	45	—
	Mean	—	—	1.1	—	0.7	—	1.8	—	2.4	—	0.8	—
	SD	—	—	2.1	—	1.4	—	2.3	—	2.4	—	1.4	—

GES—General Education Students; SWD—Student with Disabilities; SD—Standard Deviation
Source: J. Cawley, R. Parmar, T. E. Foley, S. Salmon, & S. Roy, "Arithmetic Performance of Students with Mild Disabilities and General Education Students on Selected Arithmetic Tasks: Implications for Standards and Programming," *Exceptional Children*, 67, pp. 320–21. Copyright 2001 by Council for Exceptional Children. Reprinted with permission.

Teaching students with difficulties in mathematics requires that we assist them to both *know about* mathematics and to be able to *do* mathematics. *Knowing about* mathematics means that the students understand and can demonstrate the meanings and principles of mathematics and that they are able to explain and justify these meanings and explanations. It also means the students can specify the connections between various topics in mathematics along with the connections between these topics and other school subjects and activities of daily living. Being able to *do* mathematics means that the students know a variety of algorithms and means of alternative representations for mathematics and that they can utilize a variety of algorithms to demonstrate their mathematical knowledge and skill.

Two fundamental considerations are basic to knowing about and doing mathematics. First, students learn a variety of principles and meanings about each element of the content. The students should understand that subtraction focuses on the difference between two numbers (Burnham, 1849) and that a "take away" approach to subtraction is insufficient to represent the basic meanings of subtraction (Cawley & Foley, 2002). Knowing the importance of the "information set" in contrast to reliance on the "question" in a word problem is another significant consideration. A second factor is that mathematics principles and meanings can be illustrated and demonstrated using a variety of alternative representations.

Framework for Alternative Representations

The term *alternative representations* means the interactions within a system of multiple input options for the teacher combined with a system of multiple output options for the students. This formulation recognizes the need to consider both receptive and expressive options during communication that enable either the teacher or the student to adapt to those that are most beneficial or most meaningful.

Efforts to structure the interactions that take place while using alternative representations have been described by Bruner (1966), whose concern was a model that would consider the rules that governed the storage and retrieval of information. His position was that human beings utilize three forms of information exchange: *action*; *principles of perceptual organization*, which emerge from visualization; and *representation in words or language*. He used the terms *enactive*, *iconic*, and *symbolic* to classify these phenomena. A similar framework is included within the Council for Exceptional Children (CEC) Professional Standards (CEC, 1998), where the options are designated as *concrete*, *representational*, and *abstract*. We utilize a somewhat different formulation to organize the use of alternative representations. For us, the term *alternative representations* includes manipulative, pictorial or display, spoken, and written formats and the various input and output combinations and interactions that occur between and among them. As an organizer, we have long used a framework designated as *the Interactive Unit* (IU) (Cawley, Fitzmaurice, Goodstein, Lepore, Sedlak, & Althaus, 1974; Cawley & Reines, 1996) as shown in the following display.

The Interactive Unit (IU)

		Input			
		Manipulate	Display	State	Write
Output	Manipulate	1	2	3	4
	Identify	5	6	7	8
	State	9	10	11	12
	Write	13	14	15	16

On the Input dimension, *manipulate* stipulates that the teacher moves, arranges, or compiles two- or three-dimensional materials (e.g., blocks or pictures of blocks) to represent mathematical meanings or skills. *Display* indicates that the teacher shows the students a fixed picture of an object (e.g., picture of a block) or an object (e.g., a block) itself that represents a mathematical meaning or skill. Note that when the manipulative option is used by the teacher to demonstrate a concept, for example using blocks to represent a number, it is important to remove the demonstration materials (i.e., the blocks) within a second or two. Otherwise the manipulative action is masked as the blocks are now in a fixed format and represent a *display*. *State* calls for oral communication. *Write* indicates the use of written symbols consisting of letters, numerals, or other mathematical symbols. Students' outputs include *manipulate, identify, write*, and *state*, with the latter asking the students to simply point to a pictorial response.

This model, which we use in all facets of mathematics instruction differs from the models of Bruner and the CEC and in the traditional uses of alternative representations in a number of important features. Some of these are that the IU accounts for both input and output and is very flexible in its use with word problems.

The IU accounts for both input and output. It provides the teacher with an opportunity to select a number of input options by going across the row. It provides the student with a number of response options by going down any column. The teacher might go across a row and select *write* as a means of presenting the message to the student; the teacher might then direct the student down the column to *manipulate* and this will define the interaction as *write/manipulate* (i.e., cell 4).

To encourage generalization, the teacher might present one group of students with Dienes blocks; another group of students with popsicle sticks wrapped in sets of 100s, 10s, and 1s; and a third group with dollar bills, dimes, and pennies and ask that each use the materials and build a representation of $23\overline{)276}$ in a format that represents the traditional algorithm. Our experience over the years has been that the great majority of age-appropriate students can complete the item in the *write/write* interaction (i.e., cell 16), but that few students or teachers can work the *write/manipulate* interaction (i.e., cell 4). Students who learn this procedure can complete items such as $23\overline{)200 + 70 + 6}$ as an indication of a higher-order outcome, whereas other students are stumped.

The IU is also used extensively with word problems and other forms of problem-solving activities. For example, the teacher might present the students with a word problem in a written format such as "Six whales were swimming north. Two of the whales stopped swimming." The teacher would then ask the students to gather materials and build the information set as described. This would be labeled as *write/manipulate* interaction (i.e., cell 4).

After the students create the information set, and place it before the group in a fixed presentation, now referred to as a *display* because there is no action, the teacher might then say, "I would like each of you to look at the display and write the best word problem you can." The interaction would now change to *display/write* (i.e., cell 14), as illustrated below, where the teacher can use a single picture or combination of pictures. When the pictures are used in combination, the teacher has an opportunity to determine how the students integrate information from different sets.

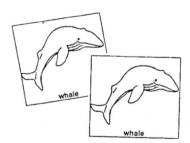
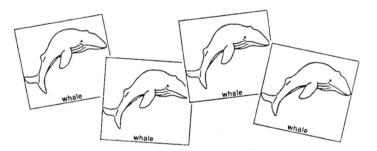

Within a single cell, or interaction, there are numerous separate tasks. Within the *write/write* cell (i.e., cell 16) alone there are up to 400 different tasks. For example, assume the teacher wanted to conduct an activity focusing on numeral recognition, number name/numeral recognition, and number concepts. A small sample of available tasks might look like the following:

In each case, the instructions are: "Look at the sample. Mark the choice that goes best with the sample."

	Sample	Choices		
a)	6	4	6	8
b)	six	4	6	8
c)	2, 4, 6	8	3	7

The three tasks, all in the *write/write* interaction (i.e., cell 16) include a match-to-sample (a) numeral matching task, (b) word to numeral matching task, and (c) concept task that involves recognition that the sample includes only even numbers and the selection of a numeral representing an even number. The interaction could readily be changed to *write/identify* (i.e., cell 8) as follows:

The instructions are: "Look at the sample. Mark the column that goes best with the sample."

Sample	Choices		
4			

The IU provides separate options for spoken input or output and written input or output. Any form of input that is composed of printed letters or numerals or of items composed of letters or numerals and specific mathematics symbols is coded as written. Students often confuse spoken and written references to numbers, yet a considerable portion of instruction in mathematics is oral (i.e., teacher explanations) and this is frequently accompanied by tasks that involve writing (e.g., textbook use) on the part of the students. It seems essential, therefore, to differentiate spoken and printed options. Further, alternative representations offer the students early access and participation in problem solving. For example, when teaching problem solving it is common to ask the students to "Read the problem" as a first step (e.g., Kleinert, Green, Hurte, Clayton, & Oetinger, 2002), a recommendation which assumes that meaningful problem solving takes place only after the students have learned to read.

The IU is not hierarchical and there is no recommended sequence such as beginning with the "concrete" and proceeding to the "representational" and on to the "abstract," the latter generally referring to symbols such as numerals. We are not familiar with any research that reports the effects of alternative sequences such as starting with the abstract and concluding with the concrete. Yet, numerous activities involving mathematics do just that. One limitation to the hierarchical model is that it fails to capitalize on the use of manipulative representations as the outcome or solution to complex problems. Within the sixteen cells of the IU illustrated earlier, ten of the cells can be used to make alternative forms of worksheets for a single concept or skill within a traditional classroom setup. Thus, the IU provides for a near unlimited number of materials. The ten worksheet-based interactions are found in cells 2, 4, 5, 6, 7, 8, 13, 14, 15, and 16. These can be used to create numerous worksheet formats as illustrated below for cell 14 (i.e., *display/write*) by having the student look at the pictures and write a word problem.

The IU enables the teacher to select a means of input and a means of output in which the students are capable. If, for example, a student has difficulty processing written symbols, the teacher can elect to present the task in another manner. The equivalence among the different cells allows the teacher to use different input and output options with different students and still measure or teach the same meaning or skill.

An examination of the processes shows a variety of mediational considerations that demonstrate common and unique characteristics between and among them. For example, both manipulative language and spoken language have messages that are transmitted in sequence as the teacher says, "Watch me" or "Listen to what I say." In both instances, the messages fade or disappear as soon as they are transmitted. Once a sentence is stated or an action performed, the student must rely on memory to review or recapture the message. By contrast, written and pictorial formats remain stable and can be reviewed when desired by the students.

Utilizing Alternative Representations in Problem Solving

Below we show a word problem accompanied by four pictures. The students are asked to mark the picture that shows the answer to the question, a *write/identify* interaction (i.e., cell 8). In effect, the pictures represent an iconic link between the iconic or display format and the symbolic form. This is relevant in that many students complete word problems without attending to the qualities of the information set and the symbolic representation.

See the clowns? Each clown has some balloons. If you take one balloon away from each clown, which clown will not have any balloons?

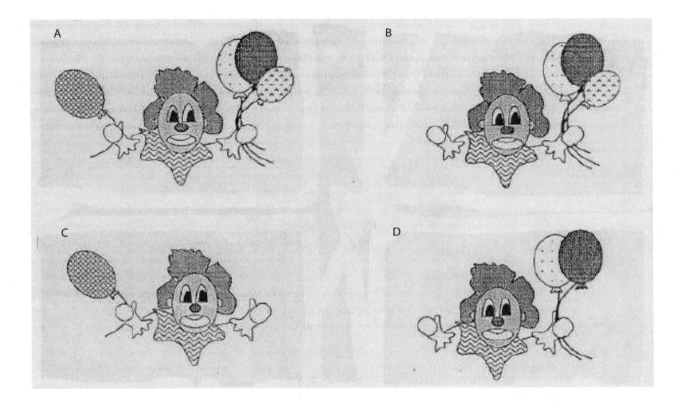

Suppose further that you gave the same word problem along with a set of materials such as pictures of clowns and pictures of balloons, and asked the students to make a representation of the problem and show the action that would give the answer to the question. Now the interaction has become *write/manipulate* (i.e., cell 4).

Or, suppose that you presented the students with a set of pictures and two word problems and asked them to select the word problem that best matched the pictures. Now the interaction has become *display/write* (i.e., cell 14).

A pod of dolphins was swimming north
Two of the dolphins stopped.
The rest kept going.
How many dolphins kept going?

A pod of dolphins was swimming north.
Two of the dolphins stopped and the rest
kept going.
How many dolphins kept going?

The key word in this activity is *best* for each of the options. What creates the basis for the selection is students' preference for one language format over another and the development of a procedure by the students to determine which of the given problems is the better of the two.

The activity could be extended within the *display/write* (i.e., cell 14) format by displaying pictures to the students and asking them to write the best possible word problem for those pictures. The students could then read their problems to one another and discuss the characteristics of each of the problems they created.

An extension of the activity might involve separating the students into small groups where they view a collection of pictures. Students can then be asked to tell a story about the pictures. Note that the pictures display different types of sea animals, mammals, and fish (i.e., *display/state*, cell 10)

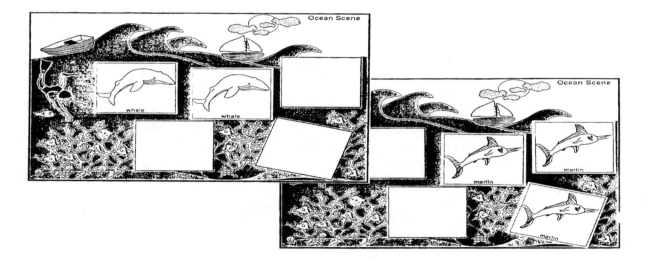

Knowing that the students have heard and can tell different stories relative to the pictures, the teacher can extend the activities by asking the students to write a story in which the last line of the story is, "The boy (girl) wondered where he (she) could find more whales so that the number of whales and the number of marlins would be the same" (i.e., *write/write*, cell 16).

What Is a Problem?

In order to understand how curricula in problem solving can be developed to enhance the mathematical reasoning abilities of students with disabilities and build on their language comprehension, it is necessary to reconceptualize what has traditionally been referred to as a "problem." To do so, we differentiate between a *problem*, an *illustration*, and an *example*, all of which have generally been treated as equivalent by prior research and curriculum development.

A *problem* is defined as an encounter with a mathematical entity for which the students *lack* an immediate course of action, *recognize* that they are uncertain about what to do, and then *ponder* or brainstorm the values of different options (consistent with Polya, 1962). Students must then select an option, implement it, determine whether the result is acceptable, and be able to illustrate and explain the basis for the selection of the option. Extensive amounts of time are needed at the problem-solving level. An *illustration* is defined as a situation where the students recognize selected components of the problem, its familiarity with previous problems, and move quickly to select an option and implement it. An *example* is where students quickly interpret an item and, with only a minimum of effort, proceed directly to a solution. With the development of increasing levels of competence, students move from the problem-solving stage to strengthening their understanding by solving illustrations, and becoming more facile and efficient by completing examples. Students must be provided with ample time to "ponder" at the problem-solving level, whereas speed and accuracy of responses should be evident at the example level.

In contrast to the typical usage of word problems in school curricula, it is important to note that the use of arithmetic word problems can give meaning to basic principles in mathematics. In fact, some form of problem solving or episodic activity is often necessary for the overall development of meaning. For example, examine the following problems:

Mary has 6 pears and wants to give each of her 3 friends the same number of pears. How many pears will each friend get?

Sara has 6 pears and wants to give 2 pears to each friend. How many friends will get pears?

Here we see the distinction between *measurement* and *partitioning* as basic concepts of division. The students can be given sets of objects and be asked to prepare a representation of each problem. They can discuss and elaborate upon the meanings of each and how they are similar and different. Additional use of the word problem to build mathematical meanings is reflected in the following problem.

Carmen bought 9 pears for 45 cents. Valencia bought 3 pears for 15 cents. Helena bought 6 pears for 30 cents. Who got the better buy?

Here, there is the need for (a) analysis and comparisons among the options, (b) activation of the process of *evaluative thinking* to decide which is the "better buy," and (c) personal interpretations as to the number of pears needed at that time or the amount of money available for the purchase. The mathematical principle addressed is *ratio*. The three word problems presented above include references to *partitioning, measurement,* and *ratio* as basic principles of division, which when explained and justified, clearly represent a higher quality of dependent variable than the answer, per se. One of the reasons we support the introduction of problemlike activities before computation is that they provide meanings for the computation. We will examine this in greater detail later on in this section.

Use of the word problem can assist students to attend to the information set of the problem and thus reduce reliance on the question. For example, a single information set can form the basis for construction of diverse questions. This encourages the students to analyze the information set for both its surface structure and deep structure meanings, rather than simply look for the given question. For example:

Harold has 6 pears in his pail. LuEllen has 3 pears in her pail.

1. How many pears does LuEllen need to have as many pears as Harold?
2. If Harold put 4 of his pears in the pail that belongs to LuEllen, how many more pears would LuEllen have than Harold?

3. If Harold and LuEllen each put 2 more pears in their pails, how many more pears would Harold have than LuEllen?
4. If LuEllen bought 3 times as many pears as she had in her pail, how many pears would she buy?
5. If LuEllen bought 3 times as many pears as she had in her pail and added them to the pears already in the pail, how many pears would she have?
6. If Harold divided his pears evenly between himself and two friends, how many pears would each of them have?

The list of possible questions is nearly endless, especially those with *if* used as a subordinating conjunction. Each question requires the students to analyze the information set in a different manner and employ different computational routines to provide a correct response. The students learn that the meaning of context is modified relative to the requirement of the task.

Information Processing in Word Problem Activities

Attention to information processing and analysis can be addressed in a variety of ways. The students can complete and discuss problems that negate the emphasis on key words (e.g., *gave, left,* and *remain* are often used as key words to subtract). To illustrate:

A boy has 6 apples left after he gave 3 apples to a friend.
A girl has 4 pears left after she gave 2 apples to a friend.

1. Together, how many pieces of fruit did the children start with?
2. Together, how many pieces did the children give away?
3. Together, how many pieces of fruit did the children have left?

One of the tactics we have used to minimize students' reliance on the question is to use the *neutral* question. The neutral question is one that does not provide the students with linguistic cues that specify the operation. For example:

The girl had 6 pears in a box. The girl added 3 pears to the box. How many pears does the girl now have in the box?

The girl had 6 pears in a box. The girl removed 3 pears from the box. How many pears does the girl now have in the box?

Note that the primary difference in the two problems is the key verbs, *added* and *removed.* The question asked in each problem is the same. Problems of the neutral-question type can be written as simple items for the first grade and complex items for the upper grades. They are a powerful technique that encourages students to address the information set and lessen their dependence on the question.

Word Problems and Conjunctive/Disjunctive Relationship

Conjunctive and disjunctive relationship can be explored with students to enhance their understanding of the commonalities and differences between and among these concepts. The following are illustrative.

1. "I will buy neither the 3 green apples, nor the 4 red apples, but I will buy 5 yellow apples," said the girl. How many apples will the girl buy?
2. "I will buy 4 red apples and 2 green apples, but I will not buy the 7 yellow apples," said the girl. How many apples will the girl buy?
3. "I will not buy the 3 red apples, but I will buy the 4 yellow apples and the 2 green apples," said the girl. How many apples will the girl buy?
4. "I will buy all 3 boxes of red apples and all 4 boxes of green apples, but only 2 boxes of yellow apples," said the girl. How many boxes of apples will the girl buy?
5. "I will buy 3 red apples and either 4 more red apples or 6 yellow apples," said the girl. How many red apples will the girl buy?

Note the ambiguity in this final example where there is more than one correct response.

Word problem activities that focus on the determination of missing information or the lack of sufficient information to complete a problem provide students with opportunities to delve into the information set. Here, the students are to examine problems of different types and to determine the information needed to complete a problem. Notice, that there is no requirement to provide an answer. In the first instance below, the *display/write* interaction shows the student a picture and requests the student to read a question and to then determine which of four options designates the form of information that is missing to complete a problem.

Teacher says, "These problems have some missing information that you need to solve the problem. I want you to tell me what information is missing. Look at the pictures. How many more bears are there than lions and tigers?"

1. The number of tigers.
2. The number of bears.
3. The number of gorillas.
4. The number of monkeys.

"How many cobras are needed to have the same number of cobras as dogs?"

1. The number of monkeys.
2. The number of cobras.
3. The number of lions.
4. The number of bears.

"If there are 3 times as many monkeys as pandas, how many monkeys are there?"

1. The number of monkeys.
2. The number of tigers.
3. The number of lions.
4. The number of bears.

"If there are 12 bears and 4 lions, how many more bears are there than lions?"

1. The correct number of bears.
2. The correct number of lions.
3. The correct number of helicopters.
4. The correct number of rhinoceroses.

Utilizing a *write/write* interaction, the teacher presents the following and asks the students to read each problem and then select the choice that designates the missing information.

1. A girl bought 6 red apples. The girl also bought some green apples. How many more red apples than green apples did the girl buy?
   What information is missing?
   a. The number of yellow apples.
   b. The name of the girl.
   c. The number of green apples.
   d. The number of red apples.
2. A boy had 6 red apples and 3 green apples. Another boy had 4 times as many yellow apples as the other boy. How many yellow apples do the boys have together?
   What information is missing?
   a. The number of yellow apples.
   b. The number of red apples.
   c. The color pants the boys were wearing.
   d. The number of green apples.

Selecting the Best Question for a Word Problem

Another activity asks the student to analyze an information set and to then select the one, or possibly more than one, choice that is the best question(s) to ask to provide an answer to the information posed. In some instances, the students may disagree and so discussion can take place.

Teacher says, "In this set of problems, I want you to tell me what you think is the best question for the problem. Some of the questions make sense and some do not. Tell me the one that makes the most sense to you."

1. A girl has 13 apples to give to her friends. Another girl has 12 apples to give to her friends. Another girl has 41 apples to give to her friends.
   Point to the best question.
   a. How many more girls are there than apples?
   b. In all, how many apples do the girls have?
   c. How many more red apples are there than green apples?
   d. How many friends do the girls have?
2. A girl has 16 green apples. The girl also has 11 red apples. The girl wants to give each of her 4 friends the same number of green apples.
   Point to the best question.
   a. How many red apples does the girl need?
   b. How many red apples will each friend get?
   c. How many green apples will each friend get?
   d. How many more green apples are there than yellow apples?

Word Problems Using Cloze Procedure

Cloze procedure is generally conducted as a reading comprehension activity. We adapted this procedure for use in sentence and story-based forms of comprehension that focus upon comprehension when it is driven by quantitative information or activities.

Teacher says, "This next set of problems asks you to fill in a missing word to complete the problem. Read the problem carefully, look at the possible answers and then point to the word that makes the answer reasonable. If you have any questions, raise your hand and I will come to help you."

1. The boy had 9 red apples. The boy _____ 6 green apples. The boy now has 15 apples.
   Point to the word that makes the answer true.
   a. polished
   b. bought
   c. sold
   d. lost
2. A girl had 7 red apples. The girl _____ 6 red apples to her friend. The girl now has 1 red apple.
   Point to the word that makes the answer true.
   a. argued
   b. painted
   c. presented
   d. purchased
3. A girl has 6 green apples. The girl _____ her apples among her friends so that each friend got 2 apples. The girl has 3 friends.
   Point to the word that makes that answer true.
   a. sold
   b. records
   c. shared
   d. ate

4. A boy had 5 green apples. A girl _____ 4 more red apples than the boy. Together, they had 14 apples.
   Point to the word that makes the answer true.
   a. bought
   b. washed
   c. sold
   d. divided

Teacher says, "In this set of problems, I want you to write in a word that makes the statement reasonable."

1. A boy has 6 red _____ Another boy has 4 red apples. Together, they have 10 red apples.
2. A girl has 4 red apples. A boy has 5 red pears. Together, the _____ have 9 red fruit.
3. A boy had 6 red apples. A girl _____ him 3 red apples. He now has 9 red apples.
4. A boy has 3 red apples. He _____ 2 red apples to the girl. The boy now has 1 red apple.

Students insert a term of their own choosing. There will be considerable variation in the responses. These should be capitalized upon to demonstrate the variations that exist in language and in individual sets of knowledge.

Problem solving is a generalized process that is an integral component of the entire curriculum. Problem solving exists when students *compare* computation items such as

$$
\begin{array}{cccc}
3 & 5 & 6 & 9 \\
+4 & +2 & \times 3 & \times 2 \\
\end{array}
$$

or

$$
\begin{array}{cccc}
6 & 4 & 3)\overline{12} & 6)\overline{24} \\
+2 & \times 2 & & \\
\end{array}
$$

to determine why two different number combinations give the same answer. Problem solving exists when students *evaluate* items such as

$$
\begin{array}{cccc}
6 & 6 & 6 & 2)\overline{6} \\
+2 & -2 & \times 2 & \\
\end{array}
$$

and *show* that four of the same number combinations produce different answers and then subsequently explain selected features of addition, subtraction, multiplication, and division. Problem solving does not ordinarily exist when students simply provide answers to items.

Views of Mathematics

Problem solving is required to determine new ways of doing things; it is required when seeking new knowledge and the ways of acquiring and modifying that knowledge; and problem solving is required when seeking new ways to make things better or to make work more efficient. Children with difficulties in mathematics seldom reach any end point in the problem-solving process.

They encounter situations where they should find new ways of doing things, but they do not do it. In effect, mathematics activities for these students always take place at a *problem* level.

Two considerations are essential in problem solving. First, students must recognize problem solving as a process that is basic to knowing and doing. Second, they must recognize that problems in mathematics include varying types of contrived and real-life problems. When viewing problem solving as a process, one must consider long-term activities that require data gathering and decision making, short-term activities that require interpretation and analysis, and situations of the present that necessitate immediate responses. As a process, problem solving must be viewed as the reason why we learn to compute.

Science is viewed as either "technology and science," where it is valued for its own sake, or as "science and society," where it is valued for its contributions and meaningfulness to society. As with science, there are similar perspectives in mathematics where mathematics is valued as having either a technology or a society focus. The mathematics and technology perspective values the role mathematics plays as a discipline and its contributions to theory and discovery. The mathematics and society perspective considers mathematics for it applications in and contributions to society. We view both approaches from a problem-solving perspective and interpret this to mean that all mathematics should have meaning and relevance to the individual and society.

Problem solving exists when students encounter items with which they are unfamiliar or situations of a complex or comprehensive character with which they do not have experience. When asked if the following can be solved in a way other than right-to-left with the traditional renaming algorithm, the student without prior experience is faced with a problem.

$$523 - 444$$

One of the major controversies surrounding problem solving and a common focus among schools is how much class time should be devoted to problem solving in proportion to time spent in computation and whether problem solving should precede computation in the curriculum sequence. We suggest that problem solving precede computation and that computation be learned as a means of solving problems. We further suggest that the proportion of time devoted to problem solving be exchanged with that presently found for computation.

Problem Solving Precedes Computation

We have presented the foregoing statement as a framework for making the case for problem solving to precede computation, recognizing there are many types of problem solving and many approaches to computation. The most overriding element of such a framework is that mathematics be understood as a process of language comprehension and information processing both within the natural language of the students and the specific language of mathematics. Students must be provided with sufficient opportunity to achieve competence with the components and processes of language comprehension and with a variety of means by which information can be processed. For example:

> The teacher says, "Look at the sentence I have written on the board. I am going to ask you to punctuate the sentences so that one set of punctuation marks will give the pears to the teacher and the other set of punctuation marks will give the pears to Helen."
>> Initial sentence: Helen said the teacher has two pears.
>> Pears to Helen: "Helen," said the teacher, "has two pears."
>> Pears to the teacher: Helen said, "The teacher has two pears."

The above can be spoken by use of intonation or written by use of punctuation marks. They represent subtle differences in the intent of the mathematics (i.e., determining who has the pears). In its original form, the sentence is an effective representation of ambiguity, and it is the relative ambiguity of the sentence that requires the students to consider both its surface structure and deep structure (Muma, 1978). Note how the ambiguity is removed with the punctuation.

Another illustration highlights the importance of the language more specifically directed toward mathematics.

> The teacher says, "Look at the sentence (i.e., equation) I have written on the board. I am going to ask you to write the sentence in two different ways so that one sentence will have an answer of 10 and the other will have the answer 11."

$$3 \times 2 + 4 = 10 \text{ versus } 3 + 2 \times 4 = 11$$

Here we note the relevance of language and the importance of language comprehension as integral to mathematics. It is essential that every lesson include a sufficient number of opportunities to ensure that each student grasps the intent of the language and that each student ably processes the information contained in the language (i.e., symbolism) to arrive at a course of action or a conclusion. Selected features of language will now be discussed under the headings of *semantics* and *syntax*. Together these present the students with numerous direct meanings for mathematics, while at the same time providing a basis upon which students must use the deep structure of the meanings to take the appropriate action or make the correct conclusion.

Semantics

Ironically, for all the attention given to arithmetic word problem solving, there is only modest attention given the full range of semantics and syntax associated with it. Wiig and Semmel (1976) state:

> In order to solve verbal problems it is necessary to first understand their nature, that is to discern the inherent relations in the problem and the processes to be applied to arrive at a solution. The ability to analyze and understand the structure of a verbal problem involves the cognition of semantic systems and general reasoning ability (p. 30).

To fully appreciate the role of semantics and syntax and their interrelationships with a variety of cognitive tasks and abilities, one has to accept the verbal problem as a *verbal problem*, rather than a computational activity surrounded by words. In effect, it is the words and their structures that create the problem. The computational component is ordinarily inserted in mathematics classes only for the purpose of providing the students with an opportunity for a contrived computational activity, not for the purpose of addressing word problems, per se. In some respects, this raises the issue as to whether or not word problem solving might be better taught in language classes than in mathematics classes.

Vocabulary is one component of semantics. Like all other facets of language, vocabulary is more fully useful to the students if it is present as a *lexical* phenomenon where each term has multiple meanings and the meanings vary within the context in which they are presented. These include the relationships between (a) nouns and verbs, in terms of subject predicate agreement (i.e., "The boys has 3 apples" versus "The boys have 3 apples"); (b) interchanges in noun/verb terms (i.e., building as a noun, building as a verb); (c) person/object/action relationships (i.e., painter/paint/painting); (d) terms modified by adjectives and adverbs; and (e) exchanges made between nouns and pronouns (i.e., The *boy* has 3 apples and 2 pears. How many pieces of fruit does *he* have?). Consider the following word problems:

The 2 girls are in the park. Each girl has 3 pails of sand. One girl added 2 more pails to her collection. How many more pails does one girl now need to have as many as the other?

The 3 boys are in the yard. Each boy has 2 piles of grass. One of the boys gave away a pile of grass. How many more piles of grass does one boy now have than the others?

The problems contain a number of elements such as:

1. Quantified reference to subject position in the first sentence (i.e., 2 girls, 3 boys).
2. Locational reference for each subject (i.e., in the park, in the yard).
3. Quantified reference to subject position in the second sentence (i.e., 3 pails, 2 piles).
4. Action statement in the third sentence (i.e., girl added, boy gave away).
5. Quantified reference to action statement in the first sentence (i.e., 2 more pails, a pile).
6. Indirect question statement (i.e., *more* implying increase, but action is difference).
7. Comparison between initial state and ending state (i.e., comparison of one girl to another, comparison of one boy to the others).

Students with mathematics disabilities who may or may not have a language disability may have difficulty assimilating the components of the problem and avoiding the modest entrapment implied when the question infers one action, but the text sets forth another.

One of the interesting features of vocabulary is that a term can have specific and direct meanings for a single incident or association or that it can involve many different meanings each of which is context dependent. Some textbooks teach a word as having a specific meaning (e.g., "divide" means "to calculate" rather than a series of generalized meanings that fit more into a lexical scheme (e.g., "divide" means (a) to separate into two or more parts, (b) to separate into different classifications, (c) to separate into opposing classes or positions, (d) to mark points on a number line, (e) to separate one room from another by means of a partition, (f) to find out how many times one number is contained in another, or (g) to describe a relationship that would require an operation that is the inverse of that typically indicated by the vocabulary used. An illustration of the latter is found in an item such as: "The boy has 6 pets. This is 3 times as many as his mother will allow him to take home. How many pets can the boy take home?" where the term "times" misguides the students who associates "times" only with multiplication.

In many instances, the students are not actually aware that when they are "dividing" they are searching for the number of instances one number is contained in another. Their emphasis is on the completion of the division item, not what it may or may not mean. A major reason for this is that students are given pages and pages of division computation without any analysis of the implications for language comprehension or information processing. This might be remedied by providing tasks such as:

"See the three items. I want you to complete each item and then draw a picture to represent the item."

$$2\overline{)6} \qquad\qquad 3\overline{)9} \qquad\qquad 4\overline{)12}$$

"I am glad you all have the items correct and that your pictures are good examples of each item. Now, let us discuss these and what each means. Notice that the answer to all of the items is the same. I asked you to draw pictures because I wanted to ask how it is that three different items and three different pictures representing each item show the same answer. Let's talk about this."

Two elements of vocabulary are important to mathematics. One element is the extent to which the students have meaningful episodic experiences while acquiring vocabulary and that these experiences provide a lexical referent of the term. That is, the experiences show the term has many meanings and also that the term may not always have the meaning implied. A second element is the extent to which the students have a variety of contextual or episodic experiences with the term so that specific meanings within a context are understood, especially when the contrived experiences of the classroom form the context for the term.

Our general approach to teaching vocabulary as an integral component of communication is to provide a variety of alternative representations generated within the Interactive Unit. Typically, we begin with the *state/identify* interaction (i.e., cell 7) because it is multilingual (i.e., teacher can *state* a term in any language) and it simultaneously provides the teacher with a number of opportunities to restate the term or to modify the context of the term without placing a burden on the students. The use of the *identify* response mode provides a safe haven for the students, as they have only to mark a picture or object within the confines of their own desks or seat area. The response of each individual student is not exposed to the group as would be the case with a *state* response. The teacher can glance at the response of each student and if it is correct, ask the student to name the item that was marked (i.e., a *display/state* interaction, cell 10). Should the teacher be working with students whose response patterns show a number of incorrect responses, the teacher can vary the number of items that provide the choices to the students. For example, as illustrated below, the number of items from which students are to make a choice can be increased from two to four (or any number, for that matter.) The basic set of information and question remained the same. The figure below illustrates one item in which the students' papers offer a two-, three-, or four-choice exemplar in the *state/identify* interaction (i.e., cell 7).

The teacher says: "One clown has some balloons. Another clown has some balloons. If one balloon was taken from each clown, which clown would have 3 balloons?"

The task can be extended to four pictures and conducted in the following way:

The teacher says: "One clown has some balloons. Another clown has some balloons. Another clown has some balloons. (Three-choice option.) Another clown has some balloons. (Four-choice option.) If one balloon was taken from each clown, which clown would have three balloons?"

The display for the four-choice activity might look like the following:

Active and Passive Problem Solving. The great majority of activities throughout arithmetic are passive in character; for example, an item is presented to a student and the student passively writes a response. By contrast, a fewer number of activities that require active participation on the part of the student are included. Our own work has focused extensively on counteracting passive learning by developing a variety of activities to engage the student. The following are illustrative.

Problem to Match the Question. The students are presented with a question such as:

"How many more apples does Felix have in his basket than Alice has in her basket?"

The students are asked to write a word problem that is appropriate for that question. Upon completion of the task, selected students are asked to write their problems on the board and comparisons and discussions are undertaken.

Information Sets to Complete a Problem Activity. These activities take place when text-formatted stories are the basis of the problem activity. The student is presented with a statement such as:

Felix and Alice were overjoyed that they finally had the 12 pieces of fruit they needed for the pie.

The students are asked to write a short story about Felix and Alice and to write the story in a manner that the sentence shown is the final sentence of the story. Again, selected students can make their stories available to the others and discussions and contrasts undertaken.

Display Activities for Problem Creation. The students are presented with a set of pictures as shown below. The students are instructed to write three word problems that will go with the pictures. The problems shown were written by students in a third-grade classroom as they are reproduced here.

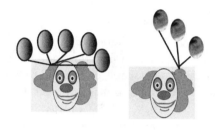

1. There was 1 clown. He has 5 ballons. He lost 3. how meny are left. A clon had 5 ballons. 4 flew away. How many did he have then
2. Thee were two clowns. 1 clown had 5 balloons and the other clown had 3 balloon. How many more balloons did the first clown have than the second?
3. A clown had 5 balloons and another had 3 balloons. How many balloons in all?

Note the variety in the use of language such as spelling, punctuation, and general sentence structure. Look further, however, and note the students created meaningful and appropriate forms of problems.

Developing Vocabulary

Vocabulary is minimally developed in three ways. One way is to provide instances or illustrations of a term and present the term. Such occurs when a name is provided for an object, an action, a modifier, or a class. This is generally a surface level approach, and little consideration is given to in-depth meanings, generalizations, or non-instances. For example, in the teaching of division, young children may be shown a few instances of a representation of division (e.g., teacher divides a set of blocks into two or more equal groups) the child is told that this is division and the division routine is introduced. The children are also told that when they hear or read the word *division* they compute (e.g., $5\overline{)25}$). The typical purpose is to teach the children the association between the operation and the term. How then do students deal with non-instances that would exist in a problem such as the following?

Louise divided her pears so that each of her 6 friends got 3 pears. How many pears did Louise start with?

In this instance the term *divided* only describes an act performed by Louise and it does not establish a relationship to division as calculation, per se.

A second approach to vocabulary development involves the students in activities that establish relationships among content, meanings, and processes. This may consist of a game, a carefully developed "hands-on" activity, or an informal activity. Students might work with materials, compare and contrast what each is doing, or be prompted or guided by the teacher and then seek a term to label or describe their experiences. For example, the teacher might provide a set of blocks and ask the students to group them in different ways so the number of blocks in each group is the same. Depending on the combinations and the attributes of the blocks, the students might group them initially by color, shape, or size and the teacher might guide them to grouping by number. For this, 12 is a good number of blocks, for it allows different students to produce different answers (i.e., 1, 2, 3, 4, 6, 12). Contrasts between those with equal and unequal numbered groups could be made and the language directed toward the labels for *equal* (i.e., multiplication and division) and *unequal* (i.e., counting, addition, or subtraction). The students are encouraged to explore alternatives, ask questions, and present different explanations for the various outcomes. The students are encouraged to think about alternative meanings, to elaborate, and to make comparisons.

A third way in which vocabulary develops is idiopathic. We do not know all the ways in which children develop and use vocabulary. Examples of some of these constructions are the use of relatively simple terms such as "a" in "A boy . . ." or "the" in "She had the . . . ." Children create combinations and permutations of vocabulary in terms of the relationships among individual words and words in context (e.g., sentences and passages), which are unrelated to specific instances of instruction. In fact, the greatest part of an individual's vocabulary and language ability is often best explained as a function of the individual interacting with the multitude of experiences in his or her environment. How this explains failure to develop vocabulary is not clear, for we know that some children do not internalize key words that come directly from a lesson. One factor that may explain this failure is an inability to establish linkages between prior knowledge and present vocabulary and meanings. Another factor may be a lack of prior knowledge. A third factor may be an inability to activate individual rehearsal and to consciously seek to incorporate the terms into new relationships.

There are many elements of vocabulary development that are not clearly understood as students utilize language for mathematics. Among these are (a) the manner in which students develop multiple relationships and meanings for terms to provide for both inclusion and exclusion from a class or context, (b) the ways in which students prioritize the meanings they affix to various terms, (c) the techniques and strategies students use to activate language and utilize it in information processing, (d) why the language of mathematics is so difficult for some students and not for others (e.g., Is this form of language more cognitively dependent?), and (e) what the interactions are between the semantic and syntactical features of the language of mathematics that create a burden for some children.

Teaching Vocabulary. One of the advantages of teaching a vocabulary such as that associated with elementary mathematics is that nearly all terms and the relationships among terms can be presented to students and represented in a number of ways. Also, there are numerous instances of application and use. One important consideration is that vocabulary must ultimately be interpreted in context and utilized in a variety of known and unknown contexts. Thus, while students may be taught that a term such as *addition* means "join" and is represented with a common symbol (e.g., we join 3 and 2 and represent them with a common symbol, 5) there are numerous other ways in which "addition" is signaled. In a context such as in the following example, addition is implied but not stated.

> The boy had 3 pears in a basket. The boy put 5 more pears in the basket. How many pears does the boy now have in the basket?

However in another context such as:

> The boy put 3 pears in a basket. The boy now has 5 pears in the basket. How many pears were in the basket to start with?

The boy "putting" and "now having" do not signal addition but subtraction. Nor is addition called for in the following:

> The boy added 3 pears to his basket. The boy now has 5 pears in the basket. How many pears were in the basket to start with?

Of course, there are also instances in which the terms do not fit, as is found in this example:

> The boy has 5 pears in his basket. This is 3 more than when he started. How many did he start with?
>
> Or
>
> The boy has 5 pears in his basket. This is 3 fewer than when he started. How many did he start with?

Instruction in Vocabulary. Three factors guide instruction in mathematics vocabulary. First, it must be recognized that we lack a one-to-one correspondence between the name for a term and its meaning. *Division* for example, does not always mean "to divide." A term such as *congruent* designates characteristics of "same shape and size" but this must relate to objects or shapes of many different types and many different sizes. Two small circles of the same shape and size are congruent; so are two large triangles of the same shape and size; and, so are all the left fenders of a specific year of an automobile model. At the same time, we must recognize the specificity of the principles involved in a term such as *congruence*. One could not indicate that a large circle and a small circle are congruent or that a small triangle and a small circle are congruent. Ultimately, students must recognize that congruence is the basis for interchangeable parts and that is what enables us to have assembly lines or to replace the dented fender. The fact that we can examine a set of model airplanes and purchase one to buy that is in a box, is another example of congruence. Sameness can be the basis for introducing selected types of learning experiences. One example might be *oddity learning*, in which the students are asked to identify the item that does not belong. A simple illustration could be:

> "Which numeral does not belong?"   1   3   7   3   1

The choice would be the 7 because it has no matching item.

A more complex illustration would be:

"Which numeral does not belong?"   1   5   7   8   9

The choice would be the 8 because the others are odd numbers.

A second factor in vocabulary instruction is accessibility. That is, the student must have access to the vocabulary and be able to interact with numerous representations. Varying combinations that can be used to bring about language interaction in individual or group settings offer efficient means by which a teacher can organize receptive and expressive language activities. In the former, the teacher might say a word, "circle" and ask one student to walk a circle, another to identify a circle, another to say what a circle is, and another to write the word or definition. Or, the same student could do all four. In a second illustration, the teacher could show a fixed display of objects or pictures that represent the cardinal property for four (e.g., hold up four pennies) and have one student create a representation by getting four pennies, another to find a picture representing four pennies, another to tell what is being shown, and another to write an expression for the four pennies. These same combinations can be put into larger contexts in which the students engage in numerous activities and use more complex language expressions.

A third factor in mathematics vocabulary development is that students must interpret and express meanings in many ways. Students should be asked to elaborate upon and prove various meanings and principles. They should be involved in showing that they understand what is given in an information set. For example, we construct word problems according to specific language guidelines as well as arithmetic computations: addition and subtraction; single-digit numbers; past, present, and future tense; and active or passive voice. When two or three problems of these types are presented to the students and the students are asked to complete them and explain or demonstrate ways in which they are similar or different, it is clearly the arrangement of the words that creates the problems. Note that the stress is on language comprehension in a quantitative setting. It is the language that must be analyzed, not the numbers, and it is improvement in language comprehension that is the goal of the lesson.

Tense—the past, the present, and the future—and voice—the active and the passive—are integral components of language. These are also interesting components around which to construct word problems, for they propose a variety of different images of the problems. A framework for the construction of word problems that manages the relationship between tense and voice is shown below.

Tense and Voice Word Problems Matrix

	Past Tense		Present Tense		Future Tense	
	Active Voice	Passive Voice	Active Voice	Passive Voice	Active Voice	Passive Voice
Addition	1	2	3	4	5	6
Subtraction	7	8	9	10	11	12
Multiplication	13	14	15	16	17	18
Division	19	20	21	22	23	24

Examples of problems written to this pattern are as follows:

Cell 1:   A trainer put 3 lions into a cage. Another trainer put 2 lions into a cage. How many lions did the trainers put into the cages?

Cell 4:   The 3 lions were put into a cage by a trainer. Another 2 lions were put into a cage by a trainer. How many lions were put into the cages by the trainers?

Lessons conducted with problems of the type shown would generally include only two problems. A discussion of the problems would focus on the image in the minds of the students as to the actions being performed. The students would be asked to describe or act out the similarities and differences in the problems.

Students must also learn to represent meanings in symbolic formats such as graphs, tables, and written reports. These are best accomplished when the students undertake a real-life study of some topic (e.g., number of pets owned by members of the class; changes in barometer readings over a three-week period). One interesting activity for the students is that they tabulate and graph the results of their own work or that of the class. This could be the results of a biweekly math quiz and might look something like the following:

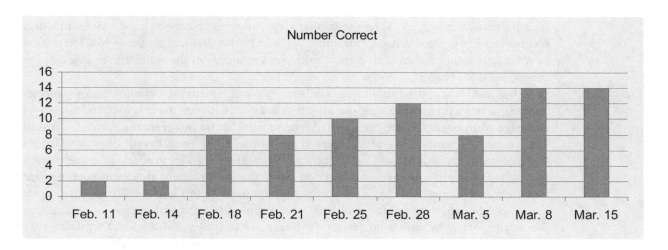

Older students could use percent correct and thereby practice an additional skill.

Syntax

A second component of language comprehension and information processing is the structural form in which terms are used. Informally, we refer to this as *grammar*, and more formally we refer to this as *syntax*. *Webster's New World Dictionary* (Neufeldt & Sparks, 1990) defines the former as "language study dealing with the forms of words and with their arrangement in sentences" (p. 257) and the latter as, "the arrangement of the relationships among words, phrases, and clauses forming sentences" (p. 599).

An examination of the word problems contained in the mathematics texts used by students indicates that little attention is given to the systematic development of word problems of varying structures with a focus on grammar. That is, the problems do not deliberately vary the grammar to provide text that modifies the meanings of words. While not an essential ingredient of programs that treat word problems as computational activities surrounded by words, grammar is an essential ingredient of a language-comprehension and information-processing approach. The former seeks a correct answer to the computational routine embedded within the problems; the latter seeks an interpretation of the meaning of the text. And, it is the latter that we believe is the foundation of successful problem solving, especially when we consider the symbolism of mathematics to be a form of semantics and syntax.

The Elements of a Word Problem

The primary elements of the word problem are the sentences. The problem typically has from one to three or four sentences that convey information. These sentences are accompanied by a question or a statement that signals a quantifying act. In most instances the students must examine two or more sentences, uncover the linkages among them, and decide which components will guide them to a solution. Sometimes the cues are direct (e.g., a term such as *remaining* suggests subtraction) while at other times the terms are indirect (e.g., a term such as *remaining* infers subtraction, but the text modifies that term and the student must add).

The sentences themselves are a composite of varying semantic frameworks and syntactical structures. The semantic and syntactical features of the word problems increase in complexity across the grades, especially as the problems are more embedded in content (e.g., problems focusing on electricity), and as new vocabulary (e.g., *amperes, volts, ohms*), and more symbolism is substituted (e.g., *v* for voltage, *i* for amperage, and *r* for resistance) for the terms. The critical concern here is that the students possess sufficient knowledge of the content to enable them to comprehend the context.

Because we support a comprehensive language-comprehension and information-processing view of word problem solving, our attention is directed toward the language and cognitive-language components of the problems. At the same time, we integrate the various forms of mathematical schemes in the preparation of problems. One scheme, that of Riley and Greeno (1988), categorizes addition and subtraction problems. It is necessary to address the preparation of problems and problem models in order to assure that the problems are of varying types and that the teacher is aware of the varying types. Our approach to this is to construct matrices that define the characteristics of the problems by any dimension or combination of dimensions deemed important by those who develop problems. For purposes of this book, a sentence is defined to mean *a set of sequenced words or terms that express a complete thought.* Integral to the sentence are the subject and the verb. The focus of the sentence is the subject and the action expressed by the sentence is designated by the verb. There are four basic sentence types, which are:

The simple sentence, which contains one independent clause.

1. A boy has 3 apples.
2. The submarine dove to a depth of 223 meters.

The compound sentence, which contains two or more independent clauses.

1. A boy has 3 apples, and a girl has 4 pears.
2. One submarine dove to a depth of 223 meters, and another submarine dove to a depth of 271 meters.

The complex sentence has one independent clause and one or more dependent clauses.

1. After the boy bought 3 apples, he bought 2 pears.
2. After the first submarine dove to a depth of 223 meters, a second submarine dove to a depth of 271 meters.

The compound-complex sentence consists of a compound sentence and one or more independent clauses.

1. The boy and the girl each bought 3 apples, and after they bought the apples they each bought 5 pears.

2. The two submarines dove to their respective depths of 223 meters and 271 meters, and after that the deeper submarine rose 86 meters.

The problem below, written as a simple sentence and a complex sentence, is modeled after one that might be found in an algebra text. This problem is usually preceded by a large number of computational items and might be the first of ten problem-solving items that include a number of items linked to a single information set (e.g., a bar graph).

1. A submarine dove to a depth of 624 feet below sea level. Ten minutes later, it is at a depth of 226 feet. What is the change in depth of the submarine?

Rewritten as a compound-complex sentence the problem would read:

1. A submarine dove to a depth of 624 feet below sea level, and 10 minutes later, the submarine rose to a depth of 226 feet. What is the change in depth of the submarine?

The text as written in the algebra book has two sentences that are connected in meaning by an extraneous information factor, "ten minutes," and by the use of the pronoun "it" to designate the submarine. When rewritten as a compound-complex sentence, the two thoughts are connected by the conjunction *and*, and the word *submarine* clarifies the ambiguity of the pronoun *it*.

Classifying Word Problems by Mathematical Constructs

As is the case with schemes used to classify problems within a language-comprehension and information-processing model, problems can also be categorized with a mathematical model. One such model (Riley & Greeno, 1988) classifies addition and subtraction problems into three general categories. These categories are *combine*, *change*, and *compare*. A few selected illustrations are shown below.

Initial item
>Harold has 3 apples. Tomasina has 5 apples. How many apples do they have altogether?

Change 1: (Result unknown).
>Harold has 3 apples. Then Tomasina gave him 5 apples. How many apples does Harold have now?

Compare 1: (difference unknown).
>Harold has 5 apples. Tomasina has 8 apples. How many more apples does Tomasina have than Harold?

Language can be modified without violating the basics of the mathematics model. For example, we can change the simple sentence problems of the Riley and Greeno model to compound sentences in the language-comprehension and information-processing model.

Harold has 3 apples, and Tomasina has 5 apples. How many apples do they have altogether?

Harold had 3 apples, and then Tomasina gave him 5 apples. How many apples does Harold have now?

Harold had 3 apples, and Tomasina had 8 apples. How many apples does Tomasina have more than Harold?

The information processing components can also be varied without violating the basics of the Riley and Greeno model. For example, the following examples use compound sentences to identify the participants (i.e., Harold and Tomasina) and their status (i.e., having apples and pears). The information-processing task is to determine the number of apples, while excluding the pears.

Harold has 3 apples, and Tomasina has 5 apples. Harold also has 4 pears, and Tomasina also has 6 pears. How many apples do they have altogether?

A modification of the above could take place by asking the following question:

How many pieces of fruit do they have altogether?

The information processing tasks now require that the students interpret "they" to represent Harold and Tomasina and "fruit" to represent the apples and pears. In both instances the students must classify both the subject and object positions of the information set. Note that while both the language complexity and the information processing required increased in complexity, the original *combine* format of the Riley and Greeno (1988) model remained intact.

The reasons for wanting to integrate a language-comprehension and information-processing model with mathematics models or schemes are threefold. First, there is broad-based recognition that students with difficulties in mathematics often have difficulties with language comprehension and information processing. In recognition of these difficulties, our belief is that activities in mathematics should address these difficulties rather than use them as a reason for the mathematics difficulties and subsequently ignore them. Second, the systematic management of language comprehension and mathematics will enable the teacher to make immediate adaptations to the needs of individuals with different types of difficulties. In some instances, the teacher might want to vary the mathematics components by presenting problems of the Riley and Greeno (1988) type combined with increases or decreases in the computational complexity in the problems. Third, the use of a comprehensive model will enable program developers to ensure the inclusion of word problems of varying structures and to ensure that a wide variety of problem types are provided across developmental levels.

CHAPTER TWO

Developing Word Problems for Diagnostic Feedback

An essential feature of mathematics programming for students with difficulties in mathematics is that the program provide the teacher with continuous diagnostic information about the performance of the students. One aspect of this is to design word problems so they provide such information. For example:

> A grocer bought 6 boxes of apples. Another grocer bought 4 boxes of soap powder. Another grocer bought 7 boxes of oranges. In all, how many boxes of fruit did the grocers buy?

The possible responses from the students are: 17, 13, 11, 10, 3, 2, and 1. Seventeen would be obtained if the students added all three numbers and neglected to exclude the four boxes of soap powder as they are not members of the set of fruit. An answer of 13 would indicate that the students conceptualized the apples and oranges as components of the set of fruit and added the 6 boxes of apples and 7 boxes of oranges to obtain the correct answer. Teachers who develop their own sets of word problems might consider the use of number combinations such as two odd numbers and one even number or two even numbers and one odd number so that each answer provided by the students would have a diagnostic referent.

An important consideration in error analysis for problem solving involves experience and accessibility. If, for example, the students cannot read and the problem is presented in a written format, it is possible the students never accessed the problem. Therefore, we know nothing about their problem-solving performance. A second consideration is experience. If the students have no experience with problem solving, the principle of error analysis may not be valid for a specific problem type.

Problem Solving, Cognition, and Language Complexity

This section on problem solving describes arithmetic problems with whole numbers of three types. One type is the traditional three- or four-sentence type of word problem. A second type demonstrates how the word problem format can be integrated with selected cognitive theories to provide direct opportunities to enhance the cognitive development of the students within the framework of arithmetic with whole numbers. The third type illustrates the use of long-term problem-solving activities to provide connections between the arithmetic of whole numbers and meaningful activities that stress social growth and development.

Word-Problem-Solving Activities

We begin the development of activities that focus on arithmetic problems of varying types with the creation of matrices. A matrix is a system by which the developer controls and specifies the characteristics of the problems. The purpose in creating matrices is to ensure that the problems created over the span of the school years will reflect a developmental progression that will cover all types of problems deemed important by the developer. For example, should the developer be a curriculum committee from a local school district, the participants would first decide the types of problems they wish to include. This might begin with word problems composed of simple sentences that use simple computation, as shown below. As the development of the matrices takes place, the types of problems would increase in complexity by whatever characteristics the developer desired.

Cognitive Language-Based Word Problems Matrix

| Language Complexity | Simple Direct Problems | | | | | Mathematics Level |
| | Reading Vocabulary Level | | | | | |
	1st	2nd	3rd	4th	5th	
Simple Subject/Simple Object	1	2	3	4	5	Addition SD+SD
Simple Subject/Complex Object	6	7	8	9	10	Addition SD+SD
Complex Subject/Simple Object	11	12	13	14	15	Addition SD+SD
Complex Subject/Complex Object	16	17	18	19	20	Addition SD+SD

SD = Single Digit

Simple subject/Simple object: Name of subject position is the same throughout/Name of object position is the same throughout

> Cell 1: A **fisherman** saw 3 **whales**. Another **fisherman** saw 3 **whales**. Together, how many **whales** did the **fishermen** see?

Simple subject/Complex object: Name of subject position is the same throughout/Name of the object position changes

> Cell 6: A **fisherman** saw 3 **whales**. Another **fisherman** saw 3 dolphins. Together, how many **sea mammals** did the **fishermen** see?

Complex subject/Simple object: Name of subject position changes/Name of object position is the same throughout

> Cell 11: A **fisherman** saw 3 **dolphins**. A **boat captain** saw 3 **dolphins**. Together, how many **dolphins** did the **sailors** see?

Complex subject/Complex object: Name of subject position changes/Name of object position changes

> Cell 16: A **fisherman** saw 3 dolphins. A **boat captain** saw 3 whales. Together, how many **sea mammals** did the **sailors** see?

The matrix shows *direct* problems, at five *reading* vocabulary levels, across *simple sentences*, with four combinations of *classification* and one level of *computation*. Students' assignments would be organized by having students do a set of problems consistent with their respective developmental status. There can be multiple problems of any single type. Assume one student had been given problems in cells 1, 6, 11, and 16; another student assigned problems in cells 1, 2, 3, 4, and 5; and still another student assigned four problems in cell 20. What do you think the teacher has in mind for each student?

A more complex matrix is illustrated below. This matrix provides sixteen different types of problems and includes all four operations on whole numbers. We provide two examples, one for cell 1 and one for cell 10.

Complex Word Problems Matrix

| | Complex Problem Structure | | | |
| | Direct Problems | | Indirect Problems | |
	Extraneous Information	No Extraneous Information	Extraneous Information	No Extraneous Information
Addition	1	2	3	4
Subtraction	5	6	7	8
Multiplication	9	10	11	12
Division	13	14	15	16

Cell 1: A tall boy gave 3 apples to the girls. Another tall boy gave 4 pears to the girls. Another tall boy gave 5 apples to the girls. How many apples did the tall boys give to the girls?

Cell 10: A tall bear had 3 peanuts. Another tall bear had 3 times as many peanuts. How many peanuts did the second tall bear have?

This matrix provides for the development of problems of the *indirect* and *direct* types, with or without *extraneous information* across the four operations of arithmetic with whole numbers. Assume the teacher assigned a student problems from cells 1, 5, 9, and 13. She then assigned another student problems from cells 8 and 16 and a third student problems from cells 1, 2, 9, and 10. What might the teacher have in mind regarding each student?

The matrix allows the teacher to assign different combinations of problems to different students, and it codes the problems for the teacher so that a future lesson can be directly related to prior performance. This approach contrasts greatly with that found in most school texts as the problems generally vary in numerous ways and often fail to provide the teacher with diagnostic feedback. Using the case of the student above who was assigned problems from cells 1, 2, 9, and 10, and further assuming the student was correct in all instances, the teacher might then assign the problems from cells 5, 6, 13, and 14 to extend the assignment to include multiplication and division. For the student whose assignment was problems from cells 8 and 16, the next assignment for this student would likely be from cells 4 and 12 to assure the student is not misled by extraneous information.

Problem Characteristics

The problems come from a system of matrices that specify the characteristics that vary across problems. The matrices are what form the curriculum. Based on individual needs and system goals, matrices may be created as needed. The matrix illustrated below focuses on the development of problems of the *direct* type.

Direct Word Problems. Direct problems are problems in which the language meanings of the information set are consistent with the operation commonly used to solve the problem. Examples of direct problems are:

Addition: A boy had 3 pears in a basket. He added 4 pears to the basket. How many pears does the boy now have?

Subtraction: A girl had 6 pears in her basket. Her friend ate 2 of the pears. How many pears does the girl now have?

Note that each of the examples uses a *neutral question* to bring the information set to closure. The questions themselves do not assist the students to select an operation. No "cue words" such as "in all" or "left" are used. The students must read and interpret the information set to determine what to do. Examples of direct problems with extraneous information are:

Addition: A boy had 3 pears and 5 apples in a basket. He added 4 pears to the basket. How many pears does the boy now have?

Subtraction: A girl had 6 pears and 5 apples in her basket. Her friend ate 2 of the pears. How many pears does the girl now have?

In each of the illustrations, the apples are the extraneous information. The improper use of or failure to exclude extraneous information is a common error among students with difficulties in problem solving. When analyzing students' performance it is important to differentiate problems with or without extraneous information. Our work with form class, which is the study of each word element in a sentence, indicates that verbs, especially when they represent extraneous information, cause considerable difficulty for students. For example:

A boy bought 3 apples. Another boy purchased 4 apples. Another boy disposed of 5 apples. Together, how many apples did the boys buy?

Because word problems are constructed using words, and words can be structured in many different ways, there are a variety of combinations of word problems that can be constructed. For example, let us look at our initial item from addition.

A boy had 3 pears in a basket. He added 4 pears to the basket. How many pears does the boy now have?

The wording could be changed to:

A boy gave away 3 of the pears in his basket. The boy then gave away 4 more of the pears in his basket. How many pears did the boy give away? How many pears were in the basket to start with? (cannot answer)

And changed to:

A boy has 3 pears left in one basket. The boy has 4 pears left in another basket. How many pears does the boy have left in his two baskets?

Or:

A boy has 3 pears left in one basket. The boy has 4 pears left in another basket. How many pears does the boy need to make one basket have the same number of pears as the other basket?

Multiplication: A boy saw 5 pears in each basket. The boy bought 3 baskets. How many pears did the boy buy?

Division: A girl has 9 pears. She wants to share the pears equally among her 3 friends. How many pears will each friend get?

Most problems of the direct type are not problems at all because the students do not analyze and interpret the information set and make decisions. Most students seek a "cue" word and then use an operation associated with that word to select an operation. What ordinarily creates the difficulty is language comprehension and not the problem per se.

Direct problems are generally used in programs that teach computation before problem solving and are used to provide a small number of examples of the use of the computation. These types of programs do not stress problem solving. Let us examine the *indirect problem type.*

Indirect Word Problems. Indirect problems are problems in which the vocabulary and information set tend to suggest one thing, but mean another. One might make the language analogy between direct problems and surface structure and indirect problems and deep structure. It is quickly evident that anyone who has learned word problem solving in a program that was dependent on cue words (e.g., "left" means "subtract") will have difficulty with indirect problems.

A direct problem for addition is stated as:

A boy had 3 pears in a basket. He added 4 pears to the basket. How many pears does the boy now have?

An indirect equivalent for addition is stated as:

A boy added 2 pears to his basket. He now has 9 pears in the basket. How many pears did he start with?

A direct multiplication problem might be:

A girl saw 5 pears in each basket. The girl bought 3 baskets. How many pears does the girl now have?

An indirect problem for multiplication could be:

A girl has 28 pears. This is 4 times as many as when she started. How many did she start with?

Or, worded in a slightly different way:

A girl had 28 pears when she reached M Street. This is 4 times as many as when she was on G Street. How many pears did she have when she was on G Street?

Or, change only the question and we have a two-step problem:

How many more pears does she have on M Street than she had on G Street?

Although the term "times" suggests multiplication, the operation needed is division. This twisting of the terms is what creates the indirect problem.

An indirect problem for addition with extraneous information might be stated as follows:

A girl added 3 pears and 4 oranges to her basket. She now has 8 oranges. How many oranges did she start with?

An indirect problem for division might be stated as:

A girl divided all her pears so that each of her 6 friends got 3 pears. How many pears did the girl start with?

An indirect problem with extraneous information can be written as:

> A girl divided all her fruit so that each of her 4 friends got 3 oranges and 5 pears. How many pears did the girl start with?

Indirect problems require considerable visualization and representation. Students might actually play out the roles or draw pictures to illustrate the problems and then discuss the inter-relationships between the information set, their actions, and their choice of operations. Understanding the relationships within the missing addend and factor × factor = product relationships is integral to success with this type of problem. Missing addend items have combinations similar to ___ + 6 = 9; 3 + ___ = 9; or 3 + 6 = ___. Factor by factor items have combinations such as ___ × 6 = 18; 3 × ___ = 18; or 3 × 6 = ___.

Two-Step Problems. The following illustrates an organizational framework for the preparation of two-step problems.

Two-Step Word Problems Matrix

		First Step			
		Addition	Subtraction	Multiplication	Division
Second Step	Addition	1	2	3	4
	Subtraction	5	6	7	8
	Multiplication	9	10	11	12
	Division	13	14	15	16

Two-step problems require the students to complete one step, assimilate that step, and then complete another step to complete the task. The matrix shows that problems written for cell 1 would have a first step as addition and a second step as addition; those for cell 2 would have a first step as subtraction and a second step as addition. To create additional items, one need only write the first step for the problem and then write the second step. For example, to write an item for cell 15, one would write a multiplication item first and then a division step second. Such a problem might look like:

> A boy has 6 oranges in each box. He has 7 boxes. He needs to give each grocer 14 oranges. How many grocers will get oranges?

A problem reversing the steps to division then multiplication (i.e., cell 12) might look like:

> A boy had 42 oranges to share evenly among 3 grocers. After each grocer had been given his share, one asked for 4 times as many as he had been given. How many oranges did the grocer want?

A primary consideration in linking computation to problems of this type is to demonstrate how strings of items can be computed. Some of these might resemble the following:

Cell	Step 1	Then	Step 2
5	Addition (e.g., 3 + 5 = ___)	then	Subtraction (e.g., ___ − 6 = 2)
7	Multiplication (e.g., 3 × 5 = ___)	then	Subtraction (e.g., ___ − 6 = 9)
11	Multiplication (e.g., 3 × 5 = ___)	then	Multiplication (e.g., ___ × 6 = 54)

Instruction in computation should include two- and three-step items such as were just illustrated and a discussion of the similarities and interrelationships between them. For example, the students might be asked to complete items similar to 3 + 4 = ___ + 2 = ___ − 4 = ___.

Word Problems Made from Nonsense Words. Problem solving is driven by more than words, per se. At times, problem solving involves an analysis of the deep structure of the information set and the interpretation of many unknowns. Such can be found in a matrix similar to that shown below. The primary difference in this matrix is that the terms are totally unfamiliar to the students and they are required to search carefully for meaning and direction. This particular activity is appropriate for students at the seventh- and eighth-grade levels. When interviewed and asked what they did to solve the problems, students generally indicated they changed the nonsense words to words they knew.

Direct/Indirect Problems with or without Extraneous Information

	Problem Category			
	Direct Problem		Indirect Problem	
	Extraneous Information	No Extraneous Information	Extraneous Information	No Extraneous Information
Addition	1	2	3	4
Subtraction	5	6	7	8
Multiplication	9	10	11	12
Division	13	14	15	16

Cell 1: Direct Problem, Extraneous Information, and Addition
A vol kilron piwed 3 trugs to the vebwons. Another vol kilron piwed 4 sutqwues to the vebwons. Another vol kilron piwed 5 trugs to the vebwons. How many trugs did the vol kilrons piw to the vebwons?

Cell 5: Direct Problem, Extraneous Information, and Subtraction
A lund seywor mindoded 3 loftaz to the fiyho. Another lund seywor mindoded 5 loftaz to the fiyho. Another lund seywor mindoded 6 lotaz to the wewsta. How many more loftaz were mindoded to the fiyhos by one lund seywor than the other?

Cell 9: Direct Problem, Extraneous Information, Multiplication
A lund seywor koptumed 3 loftaz. Another lund seywor koptumed 2 times as many loftaz as the first lund seywor. A vol kilron koptumed 4 times as many loftaz as the first lund seywor. How many loftaz does the second vol kilron koptume?

Cell 13: Direct Problem, Extraneous Information, and Division
A rih lorumd lixed 8 gootics. A soz lorumd lixed 9 gootics. The soz lorumd vuced 3 gootics to each bulmis. How many bulmises were vuced gootics from the soz lorumd?

Problem Formats. The three formats used to present word-problem-solving activities are the (a) picture, or display, format; (b) the story format; and the (c) traditional word-problem format. Each format can be designed so that it controls each of the major variables of a problem such as language complexity, type of operation, and arithmetic complexity.

A major consideration in problem solving is that a solution for all problems is not necessarily presented symbolically. For example, "Go into the store and buy 3 cans of beans for the best possible price. Bring the 3 cans back to me." requires that the student locate the correct cans and bring them to the teacher.

Script/Display/Picture Format. A variety of problem-specific activities can be developed with picture formats. Some of these are basic concepts, addition, subtraction, multiplication, and division. Items in the picture format often require the students to attend to and extract information from the pictures in order to provide an acceptable response. Many programs include pictures, but the pictures themselves are frequently extraneous to the problem, as all the necessary information is presented to the student when the examiner speaks or the student reads. Such is not the case herein. Every picture is important. The importance of the pictures is that they represent the information set used to create the problems. The use of the pictures is guided by *indefinite quantifiers.* Indefinite quantifiers are words such as *some, few, a bunch,* or *set,* in which no number property is stated. It is the indefinite quantifier that signals the student to search for the cardinality of the information sets.

Instructionally, the same set of materials and types of problem-solving activities can be presented to students at different levels of development using picture or display formats. The teacher and the students work together to create the information sets, and all the activities within a set focus on the same topic (e.g., ocean, animal habitats, etc.). Different types of questions and exchanges are used to create the problems. The illustration below shows a single picture and the accompanying script. The heading indicates the types of information processing that make up the problems and also signals the operation. Item 1 in the illustration introduces the students to categorization (e.g., students classify whales and dolphins as sea mammals), the indefinite quantifier (e.g., some, few, many) in place of a number, and the process of counting.

Unit 4: Ocean Scene
Materials:
  1. One ocean map mat.
  2. Sets of animal cards (whale, shark, marlin, walrus), 5 of each.

Introductory Activity:
    Ask the students to imitate how they think various animals sound. Include animals such as the following: horses, marlins, whales, roosters, ducks, sharks, and mules. Modify the game: have some students make an animal noise and have other students identify the animal. If possible, play a tape of animal sounds. Introduce the words *sailor, fisherman, oceanographer,* and *environmentalist* as related to oceans.

Instructor's Script—Unit Focus
    "Do you know the song 'Old MacDonald Had a Farm'? [Sing the song one time.] Old MacDonald had some whales, marlins, and sharks. What sounds do the whales make? What sounds do marlins make? What sounds do walrus make? What sounds do sharks make? Okay, today we are going to visit a make-believe ocean [i.e., the display mat] that has all these animals [i.e., display animal cards]."
        Display 1
            No Categorization/Indefinite Quantifier/Counting
            "Let's see what types of animals are in the ocean. I see SOME
                Whales (2)
                Marlins (4)
                Sharks (3)"
        "Who can tell me the number of whales, marlins, and, sharks there are?"
        Clear mat.

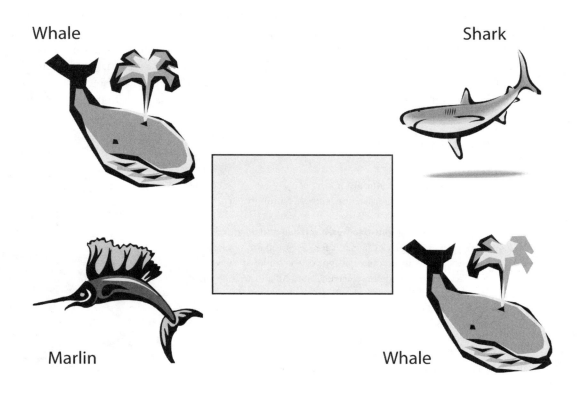

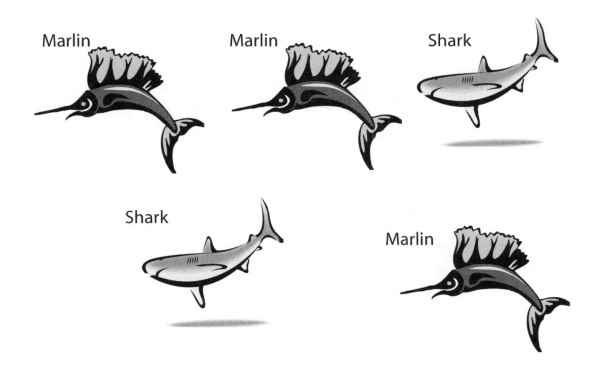

The computational requirements of each unit are identified within each display, as the illustration shows. Thus, a teacher who wants to conduct counting activities could select displays that focus on counting. A teacher who wants to introduce subtraction could select subtraction activities. The same type of materials can be used at a later time in the context of division. In this way, the students are introduced to all levels of computation within a group of problem-solving activities. The types of materials illustrated are relatively simple to create from materials in the classroom.

Unit 16: Animal Caretakers

MATERIALS

    2 zookeeper mats, 2 naturalist mats

    Sets of object cards (gorilla, lion, ostrich, flamingo, parrot, tiger)

INTRODUCTORY ACTIVITY

    Divide the group into two halves, a zoo half and a naturalist half. Have each group mark off spaces for cages and for living areas. Have each student decide what type of animal he or she wishes to be and then have them select a habitat. All zoo animals must stay in cages and all wild animals live in open areas. Have the students describe how they live to one another.

UNIT FOCUS

    Show the picture card of the male zookeeper. Say, "This is Mr. _____, a zookeeper. He and his friend, Mr. _____, (display the card of the male naturalist) each care for animals in different areas. Mr. _____ (male zookeeper) has a female zookeeper, Mrs. _____ (display the female zookeeper picture card) with whom he works in the animal habitat. (Explain term, habitat.) Mr. _____ (male naturalist) has a female naturalist, Miss _____, with whom he works (display the picture cards).

Display 1

    Display the zookeeper mats.

Set 1

    Take a set of 6 tigers and instruct a student to divide them evenly so that each zookeeper has the same number of tigers. Ask the learner to tell you how many tigers each zookeeper has. (3) (Clear mats.)

    Take a set of 4 gorillas and instruct a student to divide them evenly so that each zookeeper has the same number of gorillas. Ask the student to tell you how many gorillas each zookeeper has. (2) (Clear mats.)

    Take a set of 6 lions and instruct a student to divide them evenly so that each zookeeper has the same number of lions. Ask the student to tell you how many lions each zookeeper has. (3) (Clear mats.)

Set 2

    Take a set of 6 lions and 6 tigers and shuffle them together. Instruct a learner to take the animal cards you provide and divide them evenly so that each zookeeper has the same number of animals (the animals can be mixed in uneven combinations such as 5 lions and 3 tigers that are divided into two groups of 4). After each manipulation, ask the student to tell you what happened (e.g., I had 6 and put 3 with each zookeeper). Clear the mats after each item.

    Use the following combinations:

Give:	4 animals	8 animals	6 animals
	10 animals	2 animals	12 animals

Write Format. Note the activity below. It contains the information needed to respond to the listed questions. Note that this format engages the students in a number of questions, all relating to the same information. These fit well into discussion and brainstorming sessions relative to modification and meaning of the data set. One or two students can be assigned a given question, and students can enter into dialogue concerning the characteristics of their questions and answers. The format can include any set of content (e.g., advertisement pages from a newspaper) and accompanying questions.

Speeds of Animals

The Maximum Running Speeds of Some Animals Who Have Been Timed

Animal	Speed (miles per hour)
cheetah	70
gray fox	42
zebra	40
rabbit	35
giraffe	32
elephant	25
chicken	9

1. How much faster can a gray fox run than an elephant?
2. How much slower is a chicken's maximum running speed than a rabbit's?
3. Which can run faster—an elephant or a giraffe?
4. How much faster is the fastest animal's speed than a rabbit's?
5. If a zebra is running at 22 miles per hour, how much faster could it run if it wanted to run at its maximum speed?
6. How much faster can a cheetah run than the slowest animal that is not a chicken?
7. Which two animals have the least difference in maximum running speeds?
8. How much faster can a zebra run than the only bird on the list?

Story Format. Stories can provide the format for problem-solving activities. Each story is written in such a way that the key sets of information are quantitative. The general teaching procedure involves reviewing with students the story theme, then completing one or two questions with them, and finally asking the students to complete the remainder of the items independently. The students read a question and search the story for the relevant information. They extract the information and perform the appropriate operation. The stories can be modifications of prose the students are working with in class or they can be modifications or stories written by the students. An example follows.

Filibustering

Do you know what a filibuster is?

When a lawmaker holds up making laws by talking for a very long time, s/he is making a "filibuster." There are several examples of filibustering in the history of our country. In 1953, a U.S. senator from Oregon spoke without interruption for 22 hours and 26 minutes. He was not allowed to sit down while talking. He was speaking against an oil bill. In 1955, a U.S. senator from Texas spoke for 28 hours and 5 minutes against a bill to help water projects with tax money. In 1957, a U.S. senator from South Carolina spoke for 24 hours and 18 minutes against a civil rights act. Filibusters can take place in state government also. In 1977, a state lawmaker in Austin, Texas, talked for 43 hours against a bill. He broke the old filibuster record of 42 hours and 33 minutes.

1. Which filibuster mentioned in the story was longest?
2. Which filibuster mentioned in the story was the shortest?
3. What was the difference in time between the longest filibuster and the shortest filibuster?
4. How much longer than the senator from Oregon did the senator from South Carolina speak?
5. By how many minutes did the state lawmaker from Texas break the previous record for filibustering?
6. Who spoke for a longer amount of time—the U.S. senator from Texas or the U.S. senator from South Carolina? How much longer?
7. Which filibuster was longer—the one against the oil bill or the one against helping water projects with tax money? How much longer?

The story format is also a reading comprehension activity in which the students are encouraged to continuously search the story for needed information. Students deal with context, constantly analyze and interpret information, respond to varying information-processing demands (e.g., eliminate extraneous information), and use required arithmetic operations.

Sentence Format. The sentence format presents word problems in the traditional form of a set of three or four sentences including a question, which may be presented before or after the information set. The primary curriculum decision is the selection of the types of word problems to present. A second, and important, choice is the rationale one uses in problem solving. One rationale is that word problems are activities that *follow* computation, and the primary product of such activities is the correct answer. In this case, first-grade problems use first-grade arithmetic (i.e., single-digit computation) and fifth-grade problems use fifth-grade arithmetic (i.e., multidigit computation). Another rationale is to view word problems from a language-comprehension perspective in which the processing and analyzing of information leads to decisions or conflicts concerning that information. The language-comprehension perspective suggests that it is the words and the arrangements of the words that create problems. Thus, the content setting in which problems are presented is similar. In our work we talk extensively about boys, girls, and fruit; clowns and balloons; and animals and animal trainers. However these could be about any topic. One way to create an efficient system for adapting the problems to any content is to prepare them on a word processor and then simply use the *replace* key to substitute terms. We keep the grade-equivalent reading level of the vocabulary to a minimum. However, the teacher may increase this and the sentence complexity to any level appropriate to the developmental levels of the students. Most problems involve only single-digit computation. Yet, they *are* problems because they involve the students in the interpretation and analysis of the information set to make decisions. Again, as was illustrated, the teacher may increase this to any level appropriate. The language-comprehension view allows us to prepare problems having any set of characteristics we desire. We could, for example, prepare problems where only the vocabulary changes, as shown:

The boy ate 2 pears. The girl ate 3 oranges. How many pieces of fruit did the children eat?

The biologist illuminated 2 microscopes. The astronomer illuminated 3 telescopes. How many instruments did the scientists illuminate?

Each problem contains the simple sentences, each involves classification (e.g., pears and oranges are both fruits), each deals only with the numerals 2 and 3, and each asks the same question. They differ only in their vocabulary.

In most instances, the teacher conducts a lesson that seeks the correct answer. The language-comprehension model also seeks the correct answer, but additionally involves the students in the analysis, proof, and explanations concerning the relationship between two or more problems. In this sense, then, a lesson might only involve two to four items that are followed by extensive discussion.

Nominal Numbers

Nominal numbers are numbers that are used primarily for recording and organizing information. Nominal number activities direct the attention of the students to the use of numbers (numerals). Numbers such as a social security number, a driver's license number, or the number for a street address are nominal numbers. Nominal numbers play a substantial role in the real world as they are found everywhere and used extensively. The following example of Mr. Mizzoli illustrates an activity for nominal numbers.

Numbers, Numbers, Numbers—Nominal Numbers Example

Mr. Mizzoli got a new bank account. This new account was going to help him pay his bills and keep his records. Neither Mr. nor Mrs. Mizzoli would have to write out any more checks. The computer at the bank would do this for them. Mr. Mizzoli only had to call the bank and tell the computer at the bank the account number of the account he wanted to pay and then give the amount to be paid. These are the numbers he had:

Mr. Mazzoli's Banking Information

Telephone Number of the Bank: 401-401-7717
Personal Account Number: 658-J-7234-09-5

Bill	Account Number	Bill Amount
Electricity	65-342	$42.50
Telephone	65-777	$19.32
Rent	65-372	$750.00
Car Payment	65-1742	$340.00
Insurance	65-648	$19.63

Mr. Mizzoli got ready to pay his bills. This is what he had to do. Dial 401-401-7717. Say, "Account number six, five, eight, J, seven, two, three, four, zero, nine, five. Pay bill six, five, three, four, two the amount of forty-two dollars and fifty cents. Pay bill six, five, seven, seven, seven the amount of nineteen dollars and thirty two cents."

Mr. Mizzoli asked his wife, Louisa, to do the rest of the bills. She said, "Pay bill six, five, three, seven, two the amount of seven hundred and fifty dollars. Pay bill one, seven, four, two the amount of three hundred and forty dollars." The computer interjected and asked Mrs. Mizzoli to repeat the last item. She said, "Pay bill, six, five, one, seven, four, two the amount of three hundred and forty dollars. Pay bill six five, six, four, eight the amount of nineteen dollars and sixty-three cents. Mrs. Mizzoli hung up the phone.

Complete the following:

1. Write down the numbers of all the bills paid by Mrs. Mizzoli.
2. How much is the car payment?
3. How much is the rent payment?
4. Which bill is paid for account number 65-1742?
5. What is the account number for his insurance payment?

Although the above contains numerous quantitative tasks and activities, none of them focuses on computation. What they do is familiarize the students with a variety of "number" tasks and their interrelationships with everyday life. Tasks can be developed for any grade level, any specific students' needs, and any application of concepts and meaning about mathematics.

Organizing Quantitative Information

A multitude of quantitative concepts and meanings as well as many of the basic principles of mathematics can be used to organize, store, and retrieve information. In many instances this information is referred to as "data," and when used in this fashion it is used in basic formats, such as *average*. This information is also used in extremely sophisticated processes such as the development of economic models. Students at all levels can be presented with tasks that organize quantitative information, the primary purpose of which is to orient the students to the varying uses of quantitative information in everyday life. One such task might resemble the following:

The students are provided with the following information and asked to organize it into a chart or table.

1. During a busy week at a local automobile dealership, the dealer sold 12 four-door sedans, 9 two-door sedans, 11 one-half-ton pickup trucks, and 4 SUVs. The next week the dealer sold 8 four-door sedans, 0 two-door sedans, 6 one-half-ton pickup trucks, and 7 SUVs.
2. The teacher divided the class into four groups and asked each group to develop a table, chart, or graph that would provide a comparison between the two weeks. Each group was encouraged to be as creative as possible and to produce a presentation that would be different from that of any other group.

The key element in this lesson is the challenge for each group to be as creative as possible and to make a product that will be different from that of any other group. The final activity of the lesson will be for each group to present its outcome to the other groups and for the class to have an overall discussion of the different materials.

## CHAPTER THREE

Connections to Other Subjects

One of the key features of mathematics is the frequency with which it is used in other subjects. Nearly every aspect of daily life (e.g., setting a time for getting up in the morning), science (e.g., the weather forecast), and social sciences (e.g., reports on the AIDS epidemic) includes some aspect of mathematics. A variety of programs (i.e., GEMS, AIMS) integrate mathematics and science. A major limitation of the existing programs is that the different activities in the programs are isolated from one another and lack a cohesive sequence of developmental activities (Cawley & Foley, 2002). Our thinking on this matter, for example, is that programs that interrelate mathematics and science should be organized on a basis of mathematics and supplemented with science, as illustrated below:

Mathematics and Science Matrix

Mathematics	Science		
	Life	Physical	Earth
Counting			Determine the number of rainy days during a two-month time period.
Addition			Determine the total number of inches of rain for each week.
Subtraction			Determine the difference in the number of inches of rain in odd weeks (i.e., weeks 1 & 3) versus even weeks (i.e., weeks 2 & 4).
Multiplication			Determine the total amount of rainfall and the number of days in which the same amount of rain fell.

(Continued)

Mathematics and Science Matrix (Continued)

Mathematics	Life	Science Physical	Earth
Division			Determine the average amount of rainfall per week.
Ordinal Numbering			List the rainfall by the average amount per week from high to low.

The six quantitative operations in this activity could be utilized until the students demonstrate the designated levels of competence to whatever level of complexity, and they could also be integrated into activities within a variety of science topics.

Arithmetic Activities and Word Problems Related to Community Concerns

Addition

1. The City of New Newland has a population of 36,687. The city of Old Oldland has a population of 32,156. The cities voted to become one larger city. Together, what is the population of the new city?
2. The City of New Newland has a population of 36,687. During the month of April, a total of 251 new people moved into the city. What is the new population of the city?
3. The City of New Newland has a population of 36,687. The population of Old Oldland has a population of 32,156. During the month of September, 273 people left the City of New Newland and 185 people left the City of Old Oldland. Together, how many people left the two cities in September?

The items above provide illustrations of three meanings of addition. They are (a) joining or combining the amounts in two or more sets (i.e., item 1); (b) increasing the value of a single number by adding a number to it (i.e., item 2); (c) combining the decrease in two or more numbers to determine the value of the decrease (i.e., item 3).

Subtraction

1. The city of New Newland has a population of 36,687. The city of Old Oldland has a population of 32,156.
2. How many more people live in New Newland than live in Old Oldland?
3. How many people need to move into Old Oldland to have as many people in Old Oldland as there are in New Newland?
4. If 2,324 people moved from New Newland, how many people would there be in New Newland?

The above listed questions create items that direct themselves to different forms of subtraction and direct the student back to the same set of information each time. These are (a) What is the difference between two numbers (i.e., question 1)? (b) What number must be added to one number to make it as large as another number (i.e., question 2)? (c) What remains of a number after part of it has been taken away (i.e., question 3)?

Comparisons could be made between the two by contrasting the characteristics of two indirect problem formats such as:

The city of New Newland has a population of 36,687. The city of Old Oldland has a population of 32,156.

Indirect Addition: The city of New Newland added 267 people to its population to give it a population of 36,954. What was the original population of the city of New Newland?

Indirect Subtraction: The city of New Newland lost 267 people from its population to give it a population of 36,420. What was the original population of the city of New Newland?

The indirect addition problem signals *addition*, but the text of the problem stipulates subtraction. The indirect subtraction problem signals *subtraction*, but the text stipulates addition. Problems of the indirect type mislead the students by implying one operation while actually requiring another. It is suggested that lessons that include problems of the indirect type be limited to two problems and allow the students to devote adequate time to analyzing and comparing these problems and then explaining why the indirect problem misguides them.

Multiplication

Multiplication involves the repetition of a single set a number of times. The underlying principle of multiplication is the factor × factor = product relationship. That is, we want to know the product, or answer, when two or more numbers are multiplied by another. Word problems that focus on multiplication are often embedded in formulas that are linked to a variety of topics. As we have illustrated previously, all word problems that require multiplication do not explicitly state the act of multiplication. Foremost among these are problems of the indirect type. These problems imply division, but require multiplication. Or, they imply multiplication, but require division. For example:

Franklin ran for 3 hours. Each hour he ran 4 miles. How many miles did Franklin run in the 3-hour period?

Or:

Franklin divided his running time so that he ran 4 miles each hour for a period of 3 hours. How many miles did Franklin run in the 3-hour period?

Or:

Franklin ran a total of 12 miles. This was 3 times as many miles as he had planned to run. How many miles had Franklin planned to run?

The students are generally unfamiliar with the processes or the content from which they are constructed. For example:

Mary ran a distance of 8 miles at a rate of 4 miles per hour. How many hours did it take her to run the 8 miles?

Or:

Akwell ran 2 miles in 5 hours. If Emily ran at the same rate for 4 hours, how many miles would she run?

Or:

Katherine rode her bike 4 miles in 10 hours. If Carmela rode her bike at the same rate for 5 hours, how many miles would she ride her bike?

Students with disabilities seldom make computational errors on problems of the type illustrated, especially when calculators are used (Glover, 1993). Their errors are typically related to the context of the problem in that they do not know the content material (e.g., they do not know *rate*, *time*, and *distance* and the interrelationship among them as expressed in the factor × factor = product relationship).

Division

In contrast to the typical usage of word problems in school curricula where such problems generally serve as closure activities for computation, it is important to note that arithmetic word problems can give meaning to basic principles in mathematics aside from the direct application of computational skills. In fact, some form of problem solving or episodic activity is often necessary for the development of meaning, as was illustrated earlier in this text. For example, examine the following problems:

Michael has 6 pears and wants to give each of his 3 friends the same number of pears. How many pears will each friend get?

Or:

Luis has 6 pears and wants to give 2 pears to each friend. How many friends will get pears?

Here we see the distinction between *measurement* and *partitioning* as basic concepts of division. As illustrated previously, the students can be given sets of objects and asked to prepare a representation of each problem. They can discuss and elaborate upon the meanings of each and how they are similar and different. Additional use of the word problem to build mathematical meanings is reflected in the following problem.

Elena bought 9 pears for 48 cents. Patty bought 3 pears for 16 cents. Kimberly bought 6 pears for 32 cents. Who got the better buy?

Here, there is the need for (a) analysis and comparisons among the options, (b) activation of the process of *evaluative thinking* to decide which is the "better buy," and (c) personal interpretations as to the number of pears needed at that time or the amount of money available for the purchase. The mathematical principle addressed is *ratio*. The three word problems presented above include references to *partitioning*, *measurement*, and *ratio* as basic principles of division, which when explained and justified, clearly represent a higher quality of dependent variables to consider in intervention studies.

Quantitative and Qualitative Distractors

Extraneous information is typically inserted in word problems as either a qualitative or quantitative distractor. As a qualitative distractor, the extraneous information is generally a subject, object, or verb. As a quantitative distractor, the extraneous information is represented by a number that is irrelevant to the problem, and this requires the inclusion of a display or pictorial format. For example:

Qualitative Distractor: One group of scientists observed a group of 12 marlins. Another group of scientists observed a group of 16 whales. Another group of scientists observed a group of 8 marlins. In all, how many fish were observed by the scientists?

Quantitative Distractor: One group of scientists observed 12 marlins. Another group of scientists observed a group of 16 whales. Another group of scientists observed a group of 8 marlins. Together, how many animals were observed by the scientists who observed the 16 whales and the 8 marlins?

In the problem with the qualitative distractor, the question calls for the number of fish, which means the whales are excluded because whales are mammals. In the problem with the quantitative distractor, the 12 marlins are excluded because the question calls for the 8 marlins and 16 whales and excludes the set of 12 marlins. Attention to detail and the identification of the relevant information for processing is an essential element when contrasting these types of problems. The lesson could be extended to subtraction by posing a different set of queries.

Qualitative Distractor: One group of scientists observed a group of 12 marlins. Another group of scientists observed a group of 16 whales. Another group of scientists observed a group of 8 marlins. How many more marlins were observed by one group of scientists than by another group of scientists?

Quantitative Distractor: One group of scientists observed 12 marlins. Another group of scientists observed a group of 16 whales. Another group of scientists observed a group of 8 marlins. How many more marlins would have to be observed by the scientists who observed 8 marlins to have as many marlins as whales?

Contiguity and Noncontiguity

Contiguity and noncontiguity play a significant role in word problems that contain extraneous information. Contiguity implies that the relevant information strings in a problem follow one another without interpolated information. For example:

An oceanographer observed a set of 8 whales. Another oceanographer observed a set of 6 walruses. Another oceanographer observed a set of 11 marlins. Together, how many sea mammals did the oceanographers observe?

By contrast, noncontiguity implies that the relevant sets are separated by a set of intervening information.

An oceanographer observed a set of 8 whales. Another oceanographer observed a set of 11 marlins. Another oceanographer observed a set of 6 walruses. Together, how many sea mammals did the oceanographers observe?

The set with contiguous information is less likely to cause confusion among students with difficulties in mathematics. The problem constructed in a noncontiguous fashion causes greater difficulty for the students simply because they fail to link the relevant information.

Definite and Indefinite Quantifiers

The control of *definite* and *indefinite* quantifiers in a word problem enables the developer to heighten the attention of the students to the information set in contrast to the question. This aids the students in that they are accustomed to problems in which the question cues the operation. By combining the use of indefinite and definite quantifiers with the *neutral question*, students can be provided with problems that require their full attention to the information set, which requires that they comprehend the language of the problem and that they process information in an orderly manner. Definite problem types present the quantitative information directly. Problems of the indefinite quantifier type do not include quantitative information. Problems of the indefinite quantifier type require the use of pictures or other means by which the information is displayed. To illustrate:

Definite Quantifier: A clown has 3 balloons. If another clown has 3 times as many balloons, how many balloons does the second clown have?

Indefinite Quantifier: A clown has some balloons. If another clown has 3 times as many balloons, how many balloons does the other clown have?

Word Problems to Address Emotions

One of the key aspects of mathematics and students with difficulties in mathematics is that the activities meet both the needs of the students in mathematics as well as their needs in a variety of other areas. One of the areas in which the students can encounter difficulties is *affect*. In this context, the term *affect* refers to a host of feelings about self and others and about the situations experienced by the self and others. These experiences can be created directly by using school-type data that could include data on discipline citations, truancy, or other related acts. The problem can be posed to the students, they can provide solutions, and then discuss the implications. Another approach is to use a more indirect route and to address selected problems with the use of contrived problems. The matrix below and the sample problems illustrate one such approach.

Affective Matrix

	Positive/Positive	Negative/Negative	Positive/Negative*
Additions Comparisons	1	2	3
Subtraction Comparisons	4	5	6
Multiplication Comparisons	7	8	9
Division Comparisons	10	11	12

* Order not important

Cell 1: The seals thought that having 2 fish for lunch and 3 more fish for supper was great. The walruses thought that having 2 fish for lunch and 2 more fish for supper was super.

Cell 2: The seals thought that having 2 fish for lunch and 3 more fish for supper was terrible. The walruses thought that having 3 fish for lunch and 4 more fish for supper was unfair.

Cell 3: The seals thought that having 2 fish for lunch and 3 more fish for supper was great. The walruses thought that having 3 fish for lunch and 2 more fish for supper was awful.

Cell 1 depicts two instances of satisfaction or positive thoughts about the fish given to the two mammals. Yet, one group got more fish than the other. A reasonable question to engage the students could be, "Why do you think both groups of mammals were satisfied with the fish they received when one received more than the other?"

Cell 2 depicts two instances in which both groups of mammals were dissatisfied with their respective allocations of fish even though one received more than the other. A reasonable question to engage the students could be, "Why do you think both groups of mammals were unhappy with the fish they received even though one received more than the other?"

Cell 3 depicts a positive and a negative reaction to the number of fish received by one group in contrast to the other even though each received the same number of fish. The students could be engaged by asking the question, "Why do you think the seals were satisfied with the number of fish they received and the walruses were unhappy with the number they received?" A slight modification in the number of fish given to the walruses so that they have more fish than the seals may elicit another set of responses from the students.

This section has described a variety of word problems. Those presented illustrate only a small portion of the number and variety of types of word problems that can be developed for varying purposes. This next section will illustrate the development of word problems within the framework of two models of cognition. What is to be illustrated can be done with any cognitive model and we urge the reader to consider those that are of personal interest or interest to the district.

Formula Types of Word Problems

As students attain competence with solving word problems of varying structures and there is confidence that they can comprehend and process the information in a given problem, it is time to introduce them to problems that focus on the use of formulas. These will be illustrated with the use of problems involving machines and formulas.

Machines and Formulas

Formulas provide a wonderful opportunity to engage students in the process of problem solving as they provide an opportunity for the teacher to present situations and then have the students conduct activities that lead to meaningful assimilation of the background and roots of the formulas. The following section is devoted to a selection of formulas related to work and machines. We have exercised liberty with respect to selected elements of the nomenclature relative to work and machines, but recognize the importance of science-specific terminology in the use of the formulas in science class. Our use is to generate activities involving the process of learning about formulas rather than learning specific formulas or their specific uses.

Work and Simple Machines

The general purpose of machines is to make work easier or to make it possible to do various forms of work that a human alone could not do. Machines are intended to do work. Work is a combination of the force on an object, often stated as the weight of an object, and the distance the force is moved. The expression for this is:

Force × Distance = Work
$f \times d = w$

Numerous activities are readily available. Some of these involve a spring scale that is attached to the object and then used to pull the object a certain distance. The spring scale determines the force that is then multiplied by the distance. Students can begin to become familiar with the concept of variables as they observe the changing weight-distance relationships (e.g., a heavier object pulled for a shorter distance vs. a lighter object pulled for a longer distance). This also provides an opportunity to highlight the interrelationships of the factor × factor = product relationship, shown in the following:

How much work is done if a 5-pound object is moved a distance of 3 feet?

5 lbs × 3 ft = 15 foot-pounds

What is the distance an object is moved if a 5-pound object requires 15 foot-pounds of work?

$\frac{w}{f} = d$ $\frac{15 \text{ foot-pounds}}{5 \text{ pounds}} = 3 \text{ feet}$

What is the weight of an object that is moved a distance of 3 feet using a force of 15 foot-pounds?

$\frac{f}{d} = w$ $\frac{15 \text{ foot-pounds}}{3 \text{ feet}} = 5 \text{ pounds}$

Machines not only provide a force to move an object over distance, they also increase the speed with which work is accomplished. Power is the amount of work done in a certain period of time. Power focuses on time and is determined as shown in the following example where the amount of work is the 15 foot-pounds calculated in the previous example.

How much power is generated if it takes 3 minutes to move a unit of 15 foot-pounds?

The relevant formula is:

$$\text{Power} = \frac{\text{Work}}{\text{Time}} \qquad\qquad \text{Power} = \frac{15 \text{ foot-pounds}}{3 \text{ minutes}} = 5 \text{ foot-pounds/minute}$$

Substituting in the formula for work, power can also be calculated by the following formula:

$$\text{Power} = \frac{\text{Force} \times \text{Distance}}{\text{Time}}$$

Students should compute power using both formulas and discuss the relationships between the two.

Horsepower is a common measure of the unit of power. The formula for horsepower is

$$\text{Horsepower} = \frac{\text{Work done}}{33,000 \times \text{minutes}}$$

indicating that horsepower requires that 33,000 foot-pounds of work is done in one minute, or 550 foot-pounds of work is done in one second. Hence the formula can also be written as

$$\text{Horsepower} = \frac{\text{Work done}}{550 \times \text{seconds}}$$

Example: What is the horsepower of a machine that does 3,300 foot-pounds of work in 5 seconds?

$$\text{Horsepower} = \frac{3,300 \text{ foot-pounds}}{550 \times 5 \text{ seconds}} = \frac{3,300}{2,750} = 1.2 \text{ foot-pounds/second}$$

Consider a more powerful machine that does 48,000 foot-pounds of work in just 5 seconds. What is its horsepower?

$$\text{Horsepower} = \frac{48,000 \text{ foot-pounds}}{550 \times 5 \text{ seconds}} = \frac{48,000}{2,750} = 17.5 \text{ foot-pounds/second}$$

The machine has a horsepower of 17.5.

Consider machines with large units of horsepower, such as an automobile, which has a horsepower rating of 155. How many foot-pounds of work does this machine do in five seconds?

Horsepower = 155 $\qquad$ 550 × 5 seconds = 2,750 foot-pounds

Students who understand the relationship between multiplication and division will readily understand that if

$$\text{Horsepower} = \frac{\text{Work done}}{550 \times \text{seconds}}, \text{ then}$$

Horsepower × 550 × seconds = Work in foot-pounds
and the solution is 155 × 2,750 = 426,250 foot-pounds work.

In a similar fashion, if students know the horsepower and the number of foot-pounds of work, they can calculate the time in seconds.

Consider another type of machine, a lever that balances on a fulcrum. Display a set of illustrations or use actual balance scales set up as illustrated below. Discuss with the students the combinations and highlight the factors that influence whether the scale is in or out of balance. Note that two scales are in balance and that one of these has two smaller objects that are about the same distance from the fulcrum. Note also that two others are not in balance and that one shows a smaller object lifting a larger object and the other has a larger object lifting a smaller object. Elicit reasons for these various outcomes. If you are using an actual balance scale, move the objects different distances from the fulcrum to highlight the extent to which different distances affect the balance. Suggest that these relationships can be worked out mathematically and proceed as follows by drawing or showing with a balance scale this display.

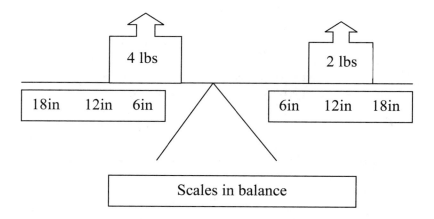

Ask: Why does this lever balance? Discuss with the students and express the result mathematically:

$$F_1 \times D_1 = F_2 \times D_2$$
$$6 \times 4 = 12 \times 2$$
$$24 = 24$$

Talk about the general rule expressed by the formula. What does it mean? If you were missing one value, but you knew the other three values, how would you find the missing value?

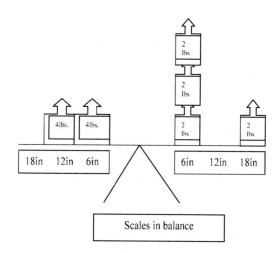

Ask: Why does this lever balance?

$$(F_1 \times D_1) + (F_2 \times D_2) = (F_3 \times D_3) + (F_4 \times D_4)$$
$$(12 \times 4) + (6 \times 4) = (6 \times 6) + (18 \times 2)$$
$$48 + 24 = 36 + 36$$
$$72 = 72$$

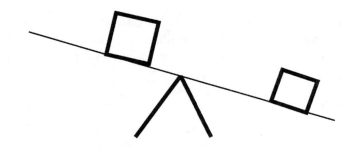

Scales not in balance.

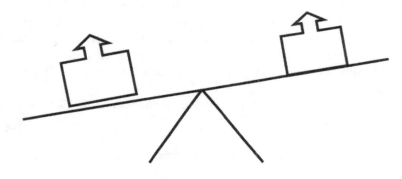

Scales not in balance.

Other formulas related to machines and work include those stating the relationship between effort and resistance, the calculation of mechanical advantage, and the calculation of efficiency.

Effort and Resistance

The formula relating all effort force, effort distance, and work input is $(W_I = F_E \times d_e)$

Effort force—the force applied to a machine (F_E)
Work input—work done on a machine (W_I)
Effort distance—distance the machine moves (d_e)

The formula relating resistance force, work output, and resistance is $(W_o = F_r \times d_r)$

Resistance force—force applied by the machine (F_r)
Work output—work done by the machine (W_o)
Resistance distance—distance an object is moved (d_r)

Mechanical advantage (MA)

$$MA = \frac{\text{Resistance}}{\text{Effort}} = \frac{F_r}{F_e}$$

Hence, if Effort = 3 pounds and Resistance = 6 pounds, then

$$MA = \frac{6}{3} = 2$$

The MA of an inclined plane can be calculated by dividing the length of the plane by its height. An inclined plane 20 feet long lifts an object 2 feet. $MA = \frac{20}{2} = 10$. And finally, efficiency (E) is the efficiency of the machine and is generally expressed as a percent $E = \frac{W_0}{W_i}$.

Pre-Algebra Thinking

We present pre-algebra thinking in the form of relationships within and among number expressions that can be represented in several different ways through the Interactive Unit (IU). One format employs the *write/identify* interaction (i.e., cell 8) and each problem includes use of the *indefinite quantifier* (e.g., some) to signal the cardinal property of the set. This requires the students to examine the pictures and solicit the needed number from the pictures. This also requires the students to backtrack the information set and determine the number for the key subject (e.g., John in problem 1) after identifying and compiling information about other persons. The response requires only that the students point to a pictorial representation. Some problems involve more than one step (e.g., problem 2 where it is necessary to determine what is 1 more than 3 times a number).

Students could be given the problems without the pictures, such as the following, and then asked to write the answer.

John has 3 pears. Mina has 3 times as many pears as John. Together, how many pears do they have?

They might also be given the problem in written form and asked to take some objects and make a representation for it. They might be given the pictures and asked to create problems for the different picture sets. Again, a variety of activities are used to communicate meanings, principles, and relationships. This also provides the classroom teacher with a means of conducting performance assessments rather than the traditional reliance on paper-pencil items.

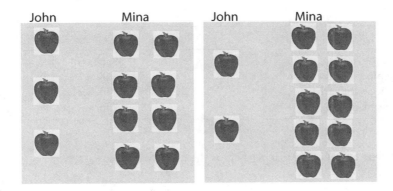

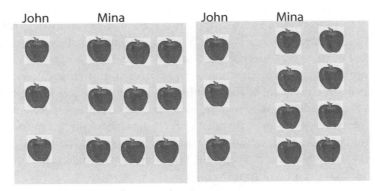

John has some apples. Mina has 3 times as many apples as John. Together they have 12 apples. Point to the picture that shows this.

Extended Problem Activities

Extended problem activities engage the student in a multiplicity of hands-on and symbolic activities to complete a series of related problems or to conduct a single long-term activity. These are illustrated in the following sections.

Related Problems

Solving a Problem. The teacher begins the problem-solving activity as follows:

"Today we are going to play the role of engineers and construction workers and make as though we are building a bridge. Many large bridges are constructed by having the builders begin construction from each side, and they then meet in the middle. The final section of the bridge is put in place to connect the two sides. You are to take a piece of cardboard and cut out pieces to match the measures on the chart. When you begin to put the pieces together you must start from the outside and glue or paste each piece as you put it together. The materials you need are on the table at the side of the room. Choose a partner and work together to complete the bridge. Here is the chart. Raise your hand if you need assistance and I will come to help you."

Building a Bridge

Chart	
Total span of the bridge	38 inches
Two outside pieces for each side	6 inches each
Two inside pieces for each side	3 inches each
Center connecting piece	2 inches

Being a Problem Solver. The teacher begins the activity as follows:

"Today were are going to again play the role of engineers and construction workers and build a bridge. As you know, many large bridges are constructed by having the builders begin construction from each side, and they then meet in the middle. The final section of the bridge is placed in the middle, and it connects the two sides. You are to take a supply of cardboard and other materials and build a bridge. When you begin to put the pieces in place, you must start from the outside and glue or paste each piece as you put it in place. Your bridge will have nine sections. I will give you a piece that is to be the middle, or final, section (many different sizes are distributed). The pieces on either side of the middle are to be two times as long as the middle piece. The pieces on the outside are to be two times as long as the pieces on either side of the middle piece. Remember, when you begin, you must start construction from the outside pieces and build toward the middle of the bridge. You may choose a partner, but it must be someone different from who you worked with on the previous task. Gather you materials. If you need any assistance, raise your hand and I will come to help you."

In the first activity, the teacher gave explicit guidelines and a list of measurements. In the second activity, the teacher does not provide any measurements or clues, except the middle piece, which is different for each set of students. The first activity involved the students in solving a problem. The second activity involved the students as "problem solvers." Both should be integral to programs in mathematics for students who have difficulty. Note that the success of the activity is a manipulate activity in which the students construct a representation of a bridge.

Problems of the type illustrated above can be used as the basis for addressing social-personal concerns among students. These could include the extent to which a student can work alone to complete tasks or the extent to which a student can work with others to complete a task. These are illustrated below.

Students Working Alone or in a Group

Teacher/Input	Student/Output
Teacher instructs the student to work independently to build a model bridge that has the dimensions stipulated in the chart.	Student builds the model
Teacher instructs a group of students to work together and build a model bridge that has the dimensions stipulated in the chart.	Students build the model
Teacher instructs the student to work independently to build a model bridge that is designed by the student and has dimensions selected by the student.	Student builds the model
Teacher instructs a group of students to work together to build a model bridge that is designed by the students and has dimensions selected by the students.	Students build the bridge

Each of the combinations provides an opportunity for a student to work independently or as part of a group and to complete a task in a manner set forth by the teacher or to complete a task of their own choosing.

Long-Term Problem Solving

Not all problem solving is short-term. Nor is all problem solving of the types described in the previous sections. The data analysis of discoveries from a ten-day mission in space begins long before liftoff and continues long after landing. Studies of the economy and weather have been taking place for many years. A bake sale at school lasts much longer than the day of the sale. Long-term problem solving should be an integral component of problem-solving activities. Problem situations can be developed for any grade level and for a topic likely to be of interest to all the students. Across the grades, long-term problem solving includes both calculations (e.g., counting for first graders; more formal statistics for seventh graders), varying formats for the representation of data (e.g., graphs), and applications (e.g., interest in a social topic such as "What do kids do with their spare time?" or a competitive topic such as compiling the win-loss records of favorite teams). These activities can be designed to focus on specific outcomes and use of the mathematical skills and context to attain these outcomes.

For example the Britannica Series, *Mathematics in Context* (Encyclopedia Britannica, 2003) consists of sets of problem-solving activities that engage the students in problem solving for an entire year. The materials for each grade level consist of a series of short softcover booklets, each of which contains a set of activities with a specific theme. For example, *Going the Distance* is a forty-six-page softcover booklet that contains a host of activities entitled "Equal Distances," "Finding Your Way," "Distances: Pythagoras," "Gliding the Distance," "Slopes and Distances," and "Distances and Areas." The lesson "Which Is Closer" presents the students with fourteen activity-based tasks and a set of summary questions. One activity shows the students a pictorial display of a campground and requires the students to determine which restroom is closer to each of four tents. Students are actively engaged in measurement and comparison. The Britannica Series provides numerous activities for students with difficulties in mathematics, and the activities are constructed in such a manner that specific disabilities of the students (e.g., reading problems) could be readily accommodated by the teacher.

As indicated in the introduction to this book we stressed the need to address problems other than mathematics, per se, during mathematics programming and instruction. When we first began our curriculum work in mathematics for students with disabilities, *Project MATH* (Cawley, Fitzmaurice, Goodstein, Lepore, Sedlak, & Althaus, 1974) we recognized the importance of long-term activities that provide applied learning experiences in mathematics. At the same time, we recognized that numerous students manifested a variety of social-personal needs that were worthy of being addressed. Programmatically, we provided a set of such activities that would enable a teacher to use only these materials for a six-year or longer period of time to address the combination of social-personal needs and mathematics principles. The following unit on temperature (page 58) shows an example of a long-term activity that focuses on the development of social skills and competencies in an activity that is structured by the mathematics. There are three key features to the units. First, the unit provides a list of selected social-personal traits that are addressed in the activities of the unit (e.g., does not begin work on time or complete assignments). The intent is that while the teacher is organizing the unit, he or she will assign tasks to students in a manner that helps address the needs of the students (e.g., completion of assignments at specific times and in specific sequences). Next, the teacher focuses on the specific quantitative concepts of the lesson and utilizes a series of probes or queries to highlight these with the students. Finally, there is a listing of the skills necessary to complete the unit. For example, it is necessary that someone be able to prepare tables and graphs. The specific skills are needed only within the group and need not be possessed by all members of the group. Thus, a student who can prepare tables and graphs would have that responsibility. An activity such as that described in the unit on temperature could be extended for an entire year, by varying the questions, organizing the data (e.g., into seasonal data), and by exchanging assignments among the students.

SUU: Temperature
Length: Two weeks; no maximum

Social Emphasis
1. Completion of assignments at specific times and in specific sequences
2. Preparation of materials and resources for analysis by others
3. Assist others with data collection
4. Participation in discussions with others

Quantitative Concepts
1. Temperature as a function of many factors such as location, time of day, and time of year
2. Temperature regulation in internal environments and in external environments
3. Quantitative predications made from acquired sets of data
4. Thermometers of different makes and styles placed in the same location to measure temperatures

Necessary Skills
1. Arranging thermometers in a given location, rotating as indicated, and recording temperature readings
2. Adding to hundreds place, subtracting numbers with up to three digits, dividing three-digit numbers by two-digit numbers
3. Preparing and analyzing tables and graphs

Introduction
This SUU may be introduced to the learners by one or all of the following activities.
1. Show pictures of individuals inside and outside a house, school, or other facility on a cold, snowy day. Link comfort level of individuals to location. If appropriate to your area, use a Polaroid-type camera to take pictures of learners, outside and inside. Use these pictures as a basis for discussion.
2. Have learners write a brief story about living conditions in some parts of the world (for example, a story illustrating living in a tropic region versus living in a polar region). Discuss stories and how people live and adapt to these regions.
3. Display pictures of air conditioners and heating units. Ask about use of them to heat or cool a beach or ski resort in order to warm the beach of cool the ski resort. Lead to discussion of outside control versus inside control.

Procedure
The emphasis in this unit is on the analysis of factors and conditions that modify temperature and, subsequently, thermometer readings. A set of four or more thermometers should be located in positions similar to the following: (a)

outside a window, (b) inside the same window, (c) inside the room near a door, (d) in a corner of the classroom, away from doors or windows.

Discuss the various activities with the learners and help them to obtain and prepare the necessary materials. These might include paper for making wall charts and graphs, pencils and pens with which to color the charts and graphs, and so forth.

Establish a daily schedule and roster for the roles. Make provisions for switching roles and tasks.

Be certain that every learner has a viable and visible role.

Work closely with the learners for a few days to ensure that all events are taking place as scheduled.

It is necessary to prepare a format for recording the thermometer readings. Something similar to that below should suffice.

Probe Questions
Do all thermometers have the same readings at the same time and location? Does the reading of one or more thermometer vary while others remain more or less constant? How do weekly graphs compare with seasons? What do we notice about Fahrenheit and Celsius levels as shown on the graph? What are the high and low readings for a given time period? What is the average temperature for a given time period?

Suggest that thermometers be rotated from one place to another. Establish a rotation schedule. Continuously plot data and introduce probe questions.

Probe Questions
Why is it that a thermometer tends to show the same measures as others in the same location? What factors seem to influence the temperature?

As the group begins to gather data, predictions might be encouraged. Do you think you can tell what the thermometer reading will be in location A (B, C, D, etc.) for the next five days? If significant variations occur, ask, "What seems to account for the change?"

Innovate as appropriate. Have the learners write stories and prepare tapes—audio and video—in roles of reporter and forecaster. Add pictures and drawings to graphs and tables.

Record of Temperature Readings
Day: _____ Time: _____ Time: _____

Location	A _____	A _____
	B _____	B _____
	C _____	C _____
	D _____	D _____

Many charts like the above will be necessary

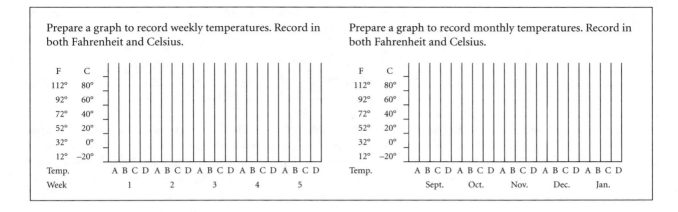

Teachers can create long-term activities of any degree of complexity and length to engage the students in the development of mathematical meanings and skills. More of these types of activities are needed in all mathematics programs.

Executive Processes

Our sense is that both teachers and students should share responsibility for the development, accountability, and evaluation of the lessons and the program. Toward this end, we developed a schemata referred to as the executive processes.

The executive processes of performance focus on those acts that are central to the completion and evaluation of the lesson. These may be referred to in some literature under headings such as metacognition or strategy utilization. The executive processes guide knowing and doing and assist students to determine the outcomes of their efforts. Instruction should begin with a plan to incorporate the executive processes into the program. This might take place in situations in which the teacher plans a series of mathematics activities for the express purpose of developing an awareness of, and responsibility for, using the executive processes.

The following is a reasonable representation of executive processes, although they may not exactly represent those that each teacher or district has in a plan.

1. Goal Setting: Do the students understand the goals of the lesson or unit? Are these presented in deductive or inductive formats? Can the students make predictions or hypotheses about the goals and set criteria for the outcomes? To what extent do the students estimate and how close to the estimations are the outcomes? Does the goal setting include procedures to activate the students and have the students review effective strategies?
2. Planning: Have you and the students worked out a plan for conducting the lesson? Do they understand the plan and what needs to be done to complete it?
3. Thinking: Will the students be provided with opportunities to think about the lesson and to think about the steps and procedures required in the lesson? Will they have opportunities to brainstorm and to share their thoughts with one another?
4. Monitoring: Is there a plan for monitoring individual and group performance and participation throughout the lesson? Do the students understand the criteria and the steps for monitoring? Can they activate prior knowledge to guide them in the monitoring process? Are they aware of techniques for self-monitoring? Will they know when to stop an action, modify the plan, and restart? Will they compare the new plan with the old plan after the lesson?
5. Evaluation: Will you and the students engage in an evaluation of the lesson? That is, will you determine that the activity was conducted successfully and that the goals were achieved? Will

the students know they are actually evaluating the lesson? Will records of their performance be an integral facet of the evaluation? Will there be discussion and elaboration on the expected data and results? Will students know how to justify and prove their outcomes and know how to restructure the lesson to achieve more effective outcomes?

6. Attitudes: Will the feelings and opinions of the students be seriously considered? What will happen if they give negative reactions to the lesson and topic?

A series of lessons could be organized to introduce each of the components of the executive processes. For example, with younger students, an activity could be introduced that centers on two word problems of different types. The students could be informed that they have two word problems of different types and that the lesson will focus on the identification of the characteristics of each type and a determination of what makes one different from the other. The expected outcome for the lesson is that each student can compare and contrast the problems and present information on their similarities and differences. Before presenting the problems, the instructor might ask the class to make a list of traits that make one problem different from another. At the beginning of the year the students might make a list of familiar traits (e.g., one is subtraction, one is addition; one has big numbers, the other has small numbers). As the youngsters become more familiar with types of problems, they might list traits such as two steps, extraneous information, and so forth. The teacher might say, "Look at the list of characteristics. Mark the ones you think will be in the problems I show you." and when the lesson is over the students can compare their "estimates" with their results.

Effective use of the executive processes requires planning on the part of the teacher and practice in application by the students. These are important facets of the program and there should be numerous opportunities for their use in both problem solving and computation.

Summary

Problem solving must be viewed as a comprehensive and dominant portion of the mathematics program. Problem solving should not be limited to the presentation of a few problems to apply a computation skill to word settings. It is clear from the analyses of word-problem types in textbooks and workbooks that the developers have not given full consideration to the language and information-processing potential of problems in the school program.

## CHAPTER FOUR

Arithmetic Computation

Arithmetic computation is a process used to compile, compare, and analyze numerical information. At a minimum it is a two-step process that necessitates *knowing about* and being *able to do* five basic operations, namely counting, addition, subtraction, multiplication, and division. Being able *to do* the operations without *knowing about* the operations is insufficient in order to be able to utilize mathematical tools (i.e., skills) in a meaningful manner. *Knowing about* each operation, that is, understanding its meaning and relationship with the other operations is essential. When instructional time is devoted to learning *about* an operation, less drill and practice is required to develop proficiency with the operation. As was illustrated in our introductory section on problem solving, knowing about problem solving requires competence in language comprehension and information processing. For example, Rose (1989) described writing and mathematics in problem solving as a process in which students or teachers write down mathematical concepts, processes, and applications as a way to explain, inform, and report. Computation is similar, as students are required to summarize actions like addition and subtraction by organizing and writing numbers in a meaningful way.

Means and Standard Deviations for Automatization Scores

Grade	3		4		5		6		7		8		
Group	GES	SWD	GES	SWD	GES	SWD	GES	SWD	GES	SWD	GES	SWD	
N	123	26	132	35	130	38	114	39	129	39	109	20	
Addition													
Mean	17.9	13.4	21.2	16.0	26.4	17.8	27.5	20.1	34.6	23.3	34.6	22.8	
SD	6.9	8.2	10.0	7.9	10.2	9.7	13.0	11.3	10.6	9.7	13.6	14.0	
Subtraction													
Mean	11.8	6.7	14.4	9.1	18.7	10.5	21.4	12.3	27.6	14.7	27.1	14.1	
SD	7.1	6.5	9.4	6.7	8.8	6.6	11.8	8.9	12.1	7.1	13.7	9.2	
Multiplication													
Mean	7.8	2.5	14.3	4.8	21.3	9.6	24.5	11.4	32.1	17.8	31.4	20.6	
SD	8.4	6.1	11.8	8.2	11.5	11.9	13.6	12.8	12.4	11.9	14.2	18.5	

(Continued)

Means and Standard Deviations for Automatization Scores (Continued)

Grade		3		4		5		6		7		8	
Group		GES	SWD	GES	SWD	GES	SWD	GES	SWD	GES	SWD	GES	SWD
Division													
Mean		3.6	1.4	9.1	2.9	16.4	6.0	20.6	7.2	27.6	9.3	27.5	15.2
SD		7.1	4.4	10.0	6.4	11.4	9.3	13.5	9.9	13.9	9.3	14.4	15.7

GES—General Education Students; SWD—Student with Disabilities; SD—Standard Deviation
Source: J. Cawley, R. Parmar, T. E. Foley, S. Salmon, & S. Roy, "Arithmetic Performance of Students with Mild Disabilities and General Education Students on Selected Arithmetic Tasks: Implications for Standards and Programming," *Exceptional Children* 67: p. 319. Copyright 2001 by Council for Exceptional Children. Reprinted with permission.

Means and Standard Deviations for Computational Proficiency Scores

	Grade	3		4		5		6		7		8	
	Group	GES	SWD	GES	SWD	GES	SWD	GES	SWD	GES	SWD	GES	SWD
Set 1 (8)	N	123	26	132	35	130	38	114	39	129	39	109	20
25 + 3	Mean	5.7	4.7	6.1	6.1	7.1	6.2	6.5	5.8	7.6	6.9	7.3	6.1
234 + 21	SD	3.0	2.6	3.0	2.6	2.2	2.5	3.1	3.1	1.4	2.3	2.1	3.2
Set 2 (8)	N	123	26	132	35	130	38	114	69	129	39	109	20
16 − 3	Mean	4.7	3.1	5.4	4.4	6.8	5.2	6.3	5.1	7.4	6.1	7.2	4.4
50 − 24	SD	3.3	2.9	3.3	3.3	2.5	3.0	3.1	3.6	1.8	2.8	2.2	3.5
Set 3 (10)	N	72	—	95	18	115	25	90	25	120	30	100	12
556 + 64 + 4	Mean	6.1	—	6.9	5.7	7.5	5.8	9.0	7.0	9.8	7.7	9.8	6.3
4,008 + 799	SD	4.5	—	4.4	4.5	4.1	4.9	2.7	4.5	1.2	4.0	1.2	4.8
Set 4 (8)	N	48	—	71	11	89	15	83	18	120	24	99	—
460 − 48	Mean	6.9	—	6.9	6.4	7.6	7.5	7.7	7.3	7.8	7.0	7.2	—
8,000 − 6,341	SD	1.7	—	2.2	2.4	1.1	1.6	0.9	1.5	0.7	2.2	1.0	—
Set 5 (4)	N	45	—	63	10	88	14	82	17	120	22	98	—
27 × 3	Mean	5.3	—	2.2	0.9	2.8	2.4	3.2	2.8	3.6	2.6	3.6	—
358 × 8	SD	1.1	—	1.6	1.4	1.6	1.6	1.4	1.8	1.0	1.7	1.1	—
Set 6 (6)	N	—	—	40	—	68	—	69	12	112	16	90	—
2 ÷ 12	Mean	—	—	3.7	—	5.0	—	5.2	5.3	5.3	4.3	5.1	—
12 ÷ 36	SD	—	—	2.0	—	1.5	—	1.4	1.2	1.7	1.9	1.9	—
Set 7 (4)	N	—	—	20	—	58	—	61	10	101	—	78	—
567 × 46	Mean	—	—	0.9	—	1.5	—	2.1	1.5	2.4	—	2.7	—
5,030 × 420	SD	—	—	1.4	—	1.6	—	1.5	1.4	1.4	—	1.5	—
Set 8 (8)	N	—	—	—	—	29	—	44	—	76	—	64	—
22 ÷ 418	Mean	—	—	—	—	6.1	—	5.1	—	6.0	—	6.4	—
348 ÷ 5,009	SD	—	—	—	—	2.6	—	2.6	—	2.2	—	2.1	—

GES—General Education Students; SWD—Student with Disabilities; SD—Standard Deviation
Source: J. Cawley, R. Parmar, T. E. Foley, S. Salmon, & S. Roy, "Arithmetic Performance of Students with Mild Disabilities and General Education Students on Selected Arithmetic Tasks: Implications for Standards and Programming," *Exceptional Children*, 67, p. 320. Copyright 2001 by Council for Exceptional Children. Reprinted with permission.

Students who are knowledgeable *about* an operation and how it relates to other operations know there are different ways to represent and many ways to carry out an operation. For example, the traditional approach to teaching the operations begins with counting and then proceeds to addition, subtraction, multiplication, and finally division. A nontraditional approach to knowing *about* the operations acknowledges that the traditional sequence may not be the only viable sequence. For example, a teacher could introduce selected principles about division before providing instruction in subtraction. This could be done as illustrated below.

Illustration A.
  The teacher displays a set of objects and asks the students to: "Make as many sets as you can with this many [points to a given number (# #)] in each set."
  The teacher displays 2 objects.   # #
  And points to an object pile.   # # # # # #
  The students separate the items in the object pile into sets of 2s.
       ##   ##   ##
  The students indicate: "There are two objects in each pile and we made three piles."

From a mathematical perspective the students have organized a set of objects into a specified number of disjointed sets without a remainder. Let us provide an illustration with a remainder.

Illustration B.
  The teacher displays a set of objects and asks the students: "Make as many sets as you can with this many [points to given number (# #)] in each set."
  The teacher displays 2 objects   # #
  And then points to an object pile # # # # # # #
  The students separate items in the object pile into 3 groups of 2 and 1 group of 1:
       ##   ##   ##   #
  The students indicate: "There are two objects in each set and we made three piles, and we have one extra object."

The teacher and students can then discuss the two illustrations in relation to their similarities and differences and why the two examples did not result in the same number of groups. This can be followed by another example that uses groups of 3.

Illustration C.
  The students are again asked: "Make as many sets as you can with this many [points to given number: # # #] in each set."
  The teacher displays 3 objects.   # # #
  The teacher then points to object pile: # # # # # #
  Students then proceed to separate items from the object pile as follows.
       ###   ###
  The students then confirm with the teacher that "There are three objects in each set and we made two piles."

The teacher can direct students' attention to the object piles in illustrations A and C and ask them to explain the similarities and differences between the two illustrations. Through guided discussion it can be noted that the number of objects in each pile and the number of piles are different. The students and teacher can then explore reasons why these differences are evident despite the fact that both Illustrations A and C began with six objects.

Once Illustrations A and C are examined, Illustration B can be added to the comparison of how B is similar or different from A and C. Inclusion of Illustration B highlights the fact that neither A nor C had "extra" objects, while B had one extra object.

Illustration D

The teacher continues with another illustration where the students are asked: "Make as many sets as you can with this many [points to given number (# # #)] in each set. Notice that you have two different object piles."

The teacher displays 3 objects.   # # #

And points to 2 object piles.   # # # # # #   * * *

The students then separate the items in each object pile into groups of 3.

          # # #   # # #   * * *

The students indicate: "There are three piles of three things each. Two of the piles have the same type of object and one pile has another type of object."

Illustration D is equivalent to the division of a two-digit number by a single-digit number (e.g., $3\overline{)63}$). Notice that throughout this activity, the teacher never stated the specific number to use for the divisor. The only reference to the divisor was in the teacher's statement "this many [points to given number] in each set." Nor did the teacher mention division. Based on these examples, it is evident that students can be taught many things to *know about* an operation that are independent of the traditional instructional sequence utilized in arithmetic.

Preparing to Compute

The majority of mathematics instructional programs do not devote sufficient attention to *knowing about* a process. For students to experience success in computation the four mathematical concepts of *counting, place value, expanded notation*, and *estimation* are essential. Each of the four concepts should be preceded by a series of activities that focus on organizational schemes of numerical information. One organizational approach utilizes patterns and sequences.

Patterns

Proficiency in mathematics requires the development of number sense, which acts as both the foundation and the mortar with which to build further understanding of mathematical concepts. Number sense is considered an emerging construct (Berch as discussed in Gersten & Chard, 1999) that involves a fluidity and flexibility with numbers. Case describes number sense as having a sense of what numbers mean and being able to mentally manipulate mathematical concepts and quantities to make comparisons in the immediate environment (as quoted in Gersten & Chard, 1999, p. 20).

Two valuable activities in the development of number sense are the pattern, or the linear tessellation, and the sequence. A pattern has two basic components: (a) the individual items or elements that comprise the pattern and (b) the *repetend*, or set of units that make up the pattern. Take for instance the following example: [1 1 2, 1 1 2, 1 1 2]. This collection of digits shows a pattern in which the items or elements (i.e., 1, 1, and 2) make a repetend. The repetend (i.e., 1 1 2) represents the specific sequence or what might be referred to in "pattern language" as an "AAB" pattern. A common verbal description might describe the sequence as "one of these (A), one of these (A) and one of those (B)." Specifically a pattern must contain a minimum of two repetends. To state it another way, each of the units must be repeated at least twice. Patterns can follow any rule that is implemented by the individual creating the pattern. There can be [AB, AB] patterns, [ABC, ABC] patterns, and so on. Utilizing numerals, an example of an AB pattern would be, [1 2, 1 2, 1 2]; while an example of an ABC pattern would be [1 2 3, 1 2 3].

Three introductory instructional activities that can be used with students are to (a) identify, (b) copy, and (c) extend a pattern. Each of these activities can be conducted at any one of three levels of cognition: (a) original learning, (b) intradimensional shift, and (c) extradimensional shift, all of which are illustrated below.

Pattern Traits: Identify a Pattern and Original Learning.

Original learning, dimension, shape, process, identify.
Pattern: The pattern is displayed for the students as shown.

The students are then asked, "Which of the examples below is the same as the pattern shown?" The students then mark the option they believe is the best choice.
The correct choice is item 3 as it represents the ABA pattern.

Pattern Traits: Identify a Pattern and Intradimensional Shift.

Intradimensional shift, dimension shape, process, identify.
Pattern: The pattern is displayed for the student as shown.

The students are then asked, "Which of the examples below is the most similar to the pattern shown?" The students mark the option they believe is the best choice.

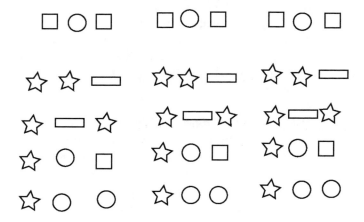

The correct choice is item 2 as it represents the ABA pattern.

Pattern Traits: Identify a Pattern and Extradimensional Shift.
Extradimensional shift, dimension pattern, process, identify.
Pattern: The pattern is displayed for the students as shown.

The students are asked, "Which of the examples below is the most similar to the pattern shown?" The students then mark the option that they believe is the best choice.

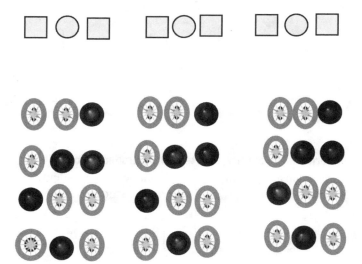

The correct choice is item 4 as it represents the ABA pattern.

The three illustrations show (a) an original learning activity in which the same elements (squares and circles) were used to create a repetend and are presented in both the sample item and the solution choices, (b) an intradimensional shift where items of the same class or concept (shapes) are substituted for elements in the sample item into the solution choices (they change from circles and squares to triangles and rectangles), and (c) an extradimensional shift where items of a different class (pattern: stripes and dots) are provided in the solution choices as substitutes for those in the class of the sample item (shape: circles and squares). The shift from original learning to the extradimensional shift is hierarchical and represents a different level of meaning for the students.

In addition to the identify or matching task, the students may also engage in copying, creating a pattern, and extending a pattern as illustrated below for the extradimensional shift only.

Pattern Traits: Copy a Pattern and Extradimensional Shift.

Extradimensional shift, dimension fill pattern, process, copy.
Pattern: The pattern is displayed as shown.

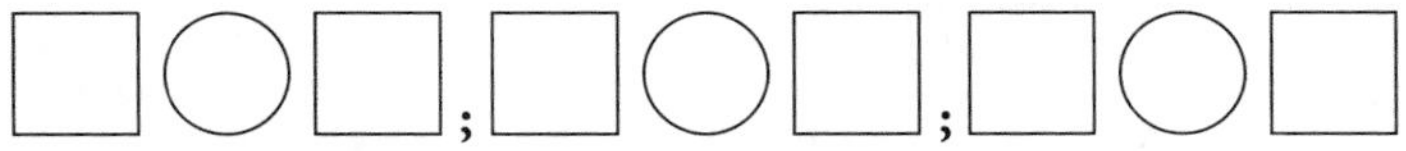

The students are then presented with a set of materials consisting of triangles and rectangles and asked to "make" a pattern that is the same as the one shown.
The correct response is an ABA pattern that would resemble either

as they both represent the ABA pattern. In effect, this is a one-to-one matching task.

Pattern Traits: Extend a Pattern and Extradimensional Shift.

Extradimensional shift, dimension fill pattern, process, extension.
Pattern: The pattern is displayed as shown.

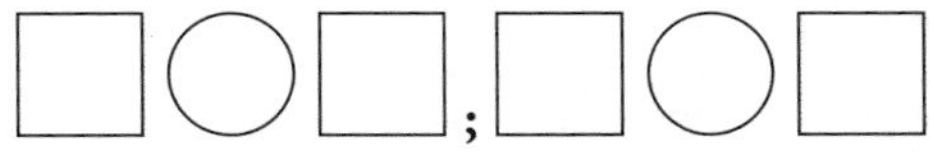

The students are presented with a set of materials that would be one of two colors (e.g., red or blue) consisting of circles. The students are asked to "make the pattern longer," or "extend the pattern." Possible correct responses from students would include:

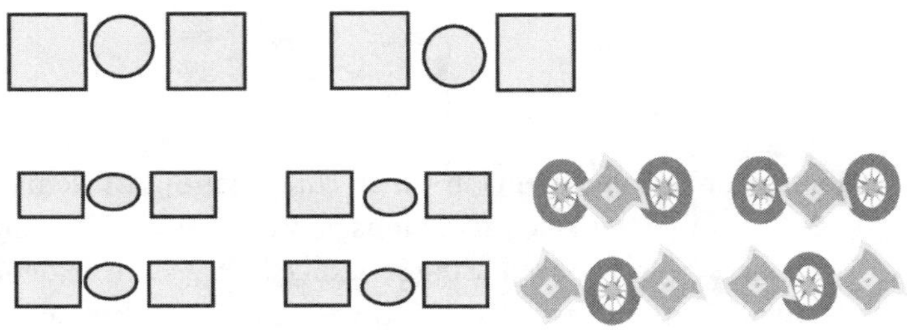

Note that this activity has two components. Students are asked to extend the pattern, and they have to extend the pattern with a different set of materials (i.e., shapes versus fill patterns). Specifically, students are asked to take a pattern that contains only squares and circles and extend it using circles that differ in terms of fill pattern. The classification of items as shapes or colors was used in these examples but any combination of materials can be used depending on the interest and ability levels of the students.

These and similar activities can be conducted with different sets of elements in a repetend, and patterns of many sorts can be used with each of the processes (i.e., original learning, intradimensional shift, or extradimensional shift). Some of the types of elements that can be used are items of various (a) shapes, (b) colors, (c) sizes, (d) objects of any kind (e.g., lions, tigers, cars, etc.), and (e) numerical properties such as number.

Pattern activities can be organized in a variety of ways beyond the linear tessellation model described above. One activity uses magic squares and missing numbers as illustrated below.

4		8
14		
		16

Ask the students to place the numbers, 2, 6, 10, 12, and 18 on the lines so that each row and column add to 30.

Ask the students to place the numbers 1, 2, 3, 4, 5, 6, 7, 8, and 9 on the lines so that each row and column add to 15.

Ask the students to select any set of numbers to create a magic square where each row and column add to a specified value.

Students should engage in a variety of pattern activities that involve the three levels of cognitive activities (i.e., original learning, intradimensional shift, and extradimensional shift) before moving on to sequences.

Sequences

Sequences are arrangements in which combinations of elements are organized in a series where students are able to make predictions about forthcoming items. It is suggested that the concept of sequences be introduced using serieslike tasks where students are given various materials with a variety of traits and asked to identify which item comes next in a specified sequence. For example, we might provide students with a set of asterisks and ask them to place the items in order from the high number set to the low number set as shown below:

Given:	***	*	*****	****	**
Response:	*****	****	***	**	*
Given:	*+*	++##	+	##	#*+*+
Response:	#*+*+	++##	*+*	##	+

Another activity uses numerals and requires students to continue a sequence by extension using a multiple-choice format.

> "Look at the sample group of numbers. From the choices that follow, select the one that will complete the sequence."
>> Sample: 112, 113, 114, ___, ___
>> Choices: A. 114, 114
>>>> B. 114, 115
>>>> C. 115, 116
>> The correct choice is C.

Note the similarity of this activity to the extension activity given above that used patterns. The primary differences between the two examples are that the elements in the sequence are not organized into repetends and the repetends are not repeated.

Activities such as the above can be followed by activities that ask the students to work with open-ended items and identify the next element(s) in a sequence, as shown below.

> "Carefully look at each group of numbers and then write the next two elements in each sequence."
>> A. 112, 113, 114, ___, ___
>> B. 123, 234, 345, ___, ___
>> C. 987, 876, 765, ___, ___

Counting

Sequences provide a variety of opportunities to engage the students in counting and related activities.

Counting Forward and Backward

Ask students to use sequence materials they are given to extend sequences A and B below. This activity represents a form of counting "on" and counting forward.

A. #   ##   ###   ####   #####   _____   _____
B. **   ***   ****   _____   _____

Ask students to use sequence materials they are given to extend sequences C and D below. This activity represents a form of counting "on" and counting backward.

C. ######   #####   ####   _____   _____
D. ********   *******   ******   _____   _____

Engage the students in a discussion about the characteristics of sequences A through D and explore possible reasons why we count both forward and backward as a way to examine the general purposes of counting.

Activities similar to the above may be conducted symbolically using numerals as illustrated below.

Provide students with sequences of numerals like those shown in sequences E and F below. Ask students to extend each sequence. Sequences E and F represent a form of counting "on" and counting forward.

E.	1	2	3	4	5	_____	_____	_____
F.	3	4	5	6	7	_____	_____	_____

Provide the students with sequences of numerals as illustrated in sequences G and H and ask them to extend the sequences to the next three elements. These sequences represent a form of counting "on" and counting backward.

G.	9	8	7		_____	_____	_____
H.	7	6	5	4	_____	_____	_____

Engage the students in a discussion of the characteristics of both sequences and solicit reasons why we count both forward and backward. Discuss the similarities and differences when counting with objects compared to counting with numerals. Highlight the fact that the use of materials and the use of symbols have a common factor in that both represent sequences based on cardinality.

Cardinal Property

A fundamental reason for learning to count is to determine the cardinal property of a given unit. In this regard, students should count everything. They can count the number of males and females in the room, the number of windows, windowpanes, and doors in the hallway. Students can count the number of desks or chairs in the room and know that the numbers of chairs and students are in one-to-one correspondence, where each chair is occupied by one student. Students should learn the number names for each cardinal set and learn rote counting. Counting can be interrelated with tallying, which can be used as a way to organize counted numbers. Students at all age levels can engage in counting activities, from the counting of single-digit numbers by young children to multidigit numbers by older children.

Skip Counting

Sequence activities with skip counting provide a background in multiplication skills where each subsequent unit increase in an item's cardinal property is related to the amount skipped. Provide the students with a collection of materials as illustrated in sequences I and J below, and ask them to use the materials to identify the next two elements in each sequence respectively. The sequences in this activity represent a form of counting "on" and counting forward.

I.	##	####	######	_____	_____
J.	***	******	*********	_____	_____

Provide the students with a collection of materials as illustrated in sequences K and L below. Ask students to use the materials to identify the next one or two elements in each sequence respectively. Sequences K and L represent a form of counting "on" and counting backward.

K.	##########	########	######	_____
L.	***********	*********	_____	_____

Activities similar to the above can also be conducted symbolically using numerals, as illustrated in sequences M and N below. Ask the students to extend each of the sequences to include the next two elements. These sequences represent a form of counting "on" and counting forward.

M. 2   4   6   _____   _____
N. 3   6   9   _____   _____

Provide the students with a sequence of numerals as illustrated in sequences P and Q below. Ask the students to extend each of the sequences to include the next two elements respectively. These sequences represent a form of counting "on" and counting backward.

P. 10   8   6   _____   _____
Q. 12   9   6   _____   _____

As the students master selected number properties and counting skills, skip-counting activities such as the above can be conducted with 5s, 10s, or any other combination of numbers.

Naming the Numbers

Two basic reasons for counting activities are to develop number sense and the words for naming numbers. Assigning numbers names is a more complicated activity than it is usually considered. Number names have both an alphabetic language and symbol formats. For example, for this symbol "2" we use the word "two" for the same symbol in "20" we use the word "twenty." The interchange between them can be confusing to many students who experience difficulties learning mathematics. The use of number names has different purposes: to express cardinality, to order quantities, and to recognize that the same number name (i.e., symbol) may represent different values, as in place value (Cawley, Parmar, Lucas-Fusco, Kilian, & Foley, 2007). When we stick to symbols, we have only ten of them plus the system we call place value to represent the infinity of number names. When we have words we have many more symbols.

Number names are first provided in a context that involves cardinal properties and are usually introduced orally. This means that when shown a set of representations, the students can name the cardinal property or numerical value represented. For example, when given items A through D below, students can respond by saying, "three," "five," "two" and "four."

Item A   Item B   Item C   Item D
####

The students must also be able to respond with, "3," "5," "2," and "4" when asked for a written response. The students may also be required to represent these combinations when they hear "three" and respond with "###," or when they see "three" or "3" and respond with "###." As the combinations become more complex (e.g., sixteen, three hundred, four) it is important that the students invoke a sophisticated level of place value knowledge to express the numbers in spoken, numeral, or object format.

Sequencing activities are excellent activities for the development of number sense and to encourage students to think about numbers and their relationships to one another. They are also excellent activities to use to develop higher-order thinking (Gavin, Findell, Greenes & Sheffield, 2000).

Reimer and Reimer (1995) provide an illustration of the relationship between numbers and their physical representation that highlights some basic principles.

An *even number* is the number of pebbles in a rectangle having two rows.

The even number 10

A *square number* is the number of pebbles in a square array.

The square number 9

An *odd number* is the number of pebbles in a rectangle having two rows with one extra pebble.

The odd number 11

A triangular number is the number of pebbles in a triangular array.

The triangular number 6

An odd number plus an odd number is an even number.

An even number plus an odd number is an odd number.

An even number plus an even number is an even number.

Eight times any triangular number plus 1 is a square number.

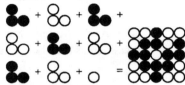

The sum of two consecutive triangular numbers is a square number.

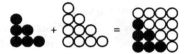

With respect to number names and the general principles of number sense, students must ultimately master the various principles of positive and negative numbers. Activities involving the number line are beneficial in this regard, especially if the number line is represented by items such as a thermometer or the daily standards of the stock market.

## CHAPTER FIVE

Knowing about and Being Able to Do

Knowing about an operation or process requires that students be able to complete items using a variety of alternative representations and a variety of different algorithms. Students should also be able to demonstrate, explain, and prove the validity of each representation and algorithm. The importance of algorithms is twofold. First, the use of alternative algorithms enables students or teachers to bypass difficulties in one step or process to attain mastery of another or to express fundamental meanings. Second, the use of alternative algorithms leads to the mastery of high-quality understanding of the meanings of mathematics principles. The 1998 yearbook of the National Council of Teachers of Mathematics (Morrow, 1998), *The Teaching and Learning of Algorithms in School Mathematics*, provides numerous illustrations of the vitality of alternative algorithms. For example, Carroll and Porter (1998) describe selected algorithms for the four basic operations of arithmetic. Kamii and Dominick (1998) suggest the direct teaching of algorithms may be harmful in two ways: first, direct instruction of alternative algorithms may encourage students to give up on their own thinking; and second, they unteach place value, thereby limiting students' development of number sense. Ginsburg (1989) discusses how students use algorithms and how some students select an alternative algorithm to complete an item, such as the case of Kathy, who was attempting to use counting to do multiplication. Kathy counted on her fingers to determine 12×6, which resulted in her finding that 10 groups of 6 made 60 and then counting on until she had 12 groups of 6. The important consideration here is that Kathy was allowed to use her own algorithm.

Philipp (1996) describes a multicultural perspective on the use of algorithms by displaying a set of algorithms used by individuals in different countries. One girl of Irish heritage showed the following for addition.

$$
\begin{array}{r}
1\ 2\ 3 \\
+\ 3_1\ 7_1\ 8 \\
\hline
5\ 0\ 1
\end{array}
$$

Ashlock (1976) examined errors made by students in computation and identified a number of error patterns, all of which are algorithmic. To illustrate, he describes an error pattern for Dorothy (p. 23) where she added the single digit number to both the ones and tens digits of the two digit number.

$$
\begin{array}{cccc}
75 & 67 & 84 & 59 \\
\underline{+\ 8} & \underline{+\ 4} & \underline{+\ 9} & \underline{+\ 6} \\
163 & 111 & 183 & 125
\end{array}
$$

In the first item, Dorothy added the 8 and 5 correctly and got 13. She carried the 1 into the 10s column, but then added the 8 from the 1s column to the 7 and the 1 in the 10s column. Although Dorothy was incorrect in how she added, her error pattern was consistent. The consistency in error patterns is something that many students who experience difficulty in mathematics demonstrate.

Selected principles of computation:

> Addition as:
> > Joining
> > Parts Equal Whole
> Subtraction as:
> > Difference
> > Search for Missing Addend
> Multiplication as:
> > Factor-by-Factor = Product
> > Distributive Property
> > One Group Many Times
> Division as:
> > Search for Missing Factor
> > One Group into Many Groups

There are two important programmatic concerns of arithmetic. One of these is the curricula choices and the other is the inclusion of alternative representations or instructional patterning. The former is generally referred to as the *content choice* and the latter as the *task choice*. Let us first examine the content choice.

Curricula Choices

Experts may agree or disagree on the sequencing of specific items within a curriculum, and in reality, professionals at the district level ought to examine any proposed sequence to assure it addresses the goals of the district. The first part of the appendix displays a curriculum sequence for addition, (sequences for all four operations are presented in the appendix).

Computational Sequence for Addition

	Examples		Descriptor
A1	6 + 3	4 + 2	Single Digit + Single Digit, No Renaming
A2	9 + 7	8 + 4	Single Digit + Single Digit, Renaming 1s
A3	6 2 + 1	3 5 + 1	Single Digit + Single Digit + Single Digit, No Renaming
A4	4 8 + 3	3 9 + 5	Single Digit + Single Digit + Single Digit, Renaming 1s
A5	36 + 3	63 + 4	Two Digit + Single Digit, No Renaming

(Continued)

Computational Sequence for Addition (Continued)

	Examples		Descriptor
A6	58 + 9	47 + 8	Two Digit + Single Digit, Renaming 1s
A7	98 + 8	94 + 9	Two digit + single digit, Renaming 1s and 10s
A8	53 + 32	35 + 52	Two Digit + Two Digit, No Renaming
A9	65 + 19	74 + 18	Two Digit + Two Digit, Renaming 1s
A10	77 + 51	83 + 64	Two Digit + Two Digit, Renaming 10s

The initial ten addition items have within them selected items in **bold** text (i.e., items A1 and A5). These items can be used as test items or queries. The items in nonbold text represent a sequence of steps between each of the items in bold text.

The sequences and the designation of items in bold text guide the use of two basic principles of curriculum usage. First, there is the principle of *proximity analysis*. Proximity analysis enables the curriculum developer or teacher to organize the components of the curriculum so that one step precedes or follows another with only a minimum of change. This enables a teacher to observe the performance of a student, assuming the student erred, and to look back and determine the prior item on which the student was successful. The teacher can examine the gaps between the previous item on which the student was successful and the item on which the student erred. Further, assume the student was successful on a given item and the teacher was preparing a subsequent assignment. The teacher could look ahead in the sequence and develop a lesson that incorporates items that introduce specific changes in their characteristics. For example, assume the current lesson was composed of items of the A6, A8, and A10 types, and that the student was successful on A6 and A8, but erred on A10. The teacher could logically conclude that the student was able to compute "two-digit plus two-digit items without renaming" (i.e., item A8) and those "with renaming" (i.e., A9) when the renaming took place within a single column. The teacher might check for details in the performance of the student by including combinations of items of the A8, A9, and A10 types. Should the student perform adequately on A8 and err on A9 and A10, then the teacher would first direct instruction to items of the A9 type.

In essence, what proximity analysis does for teachers is to allow them to make decisions about a student that are based upon the items of success and failure that are proximate to the items of concern.

A second feature of a curriculum sequence is that it provides the teacher with an opportunity to work within the principle of *least correction*. This principle encourages the teacher to restrict instruction to the precise error that has occurred so as not to engage in over correction. For example, assume a student had been given an assignment comprised of items of the A24 type, "three digits plus three digits, no renaming" and completed the items in the following manner.

$$
\begin{array}{r} 243 \\ + 146 \\ \hline 300 \\ \mathbf{70} \\ + \ 9 \\ \hline 379 \end{array}
\qquad
\begin{array}{r} 315 \\ + 273 \\ \hline 500 \\ 80 \\ + \ 7 \\ \hline 587 \end{array}
$$

The student erred on both items. In many instances, the instruction would find fault with the left-to-right algorithm and first instruct the student to start on the right and point to the 3 or 5. Actually, the left-to-right algorithm was correct. The student's error was in adding the 10s in the first problem (i.e., 40 + 40) and the 1s in the second problem (i.e., 5 + 3). The principle of least correction would stipulate that the algorithm should not be changed and that instruction should be directed to the errors of "fact."

Alternative Representations

Alternative representations are the task choices of arithmetic. Although there is considerable discussion in the literature as to the value of the use of alternative representations, we are personally committed to them as an aspect of acquiring knowledge about mathematics principles and knowledge of ways of doing mathematics. We suggest that it is as important that the students are able to demonstrate their knowledge and processing in mathematics with manipulatives as it is for them to learn to utilize manipulatives in the early stages of learning a new mathematical concept.

A long-standing framework for the organization of alternative representations is the Interactive Unit (IU) (Cawley, Fitzmaurice, Goodstein, Lepore, Sedlak, & Althaus, 1974). The IU consists of sixteen possible interaction combinations between or among teachers, materials, and students.

Interactive Unit Example with Single-Digit Multiplication

IU Descriptor	Single-Digit Multiplication
Manipulate/Manipulate (i.e., cell 1)	The teacher creates an array by placing two objects in each of four rows. The teacher cues the student by saying something like "Watch me. Make one like mine." The teacher then has the student make an array that is the same as the one he or she created.
Manipulate/Identify (i.e., cell 5)	The teacher creates an array by placing two objects in each of four rows. The teacher cues the student by saying something like "Watch me. Pick one here that shows what I did." The teacher shows two or more pictorial representations of arrays and has the student point to the one that is representative of the one he or she created.
Manipulate/State (i.e., cell 9)	The teacher creates an array by placing two objects in each of four rows. The teacher cues the student by saying something like "Watch me. I want you to tell me what I show you." The teacher then has the student tell about what is shown.
Manipulate/Write (i.e., cell 13)	The teacher creates an array by placing two objects in each of four rows. The teacher cues the student by saying something like "Watch me. I want you to write a number sentence to show what I did." The student writes a number sentence with or without an answer.
Display/Manipulate (i.e., cell 2)	The teacher shows the student a pictorial representation of a four-by-two array. The teacher cues the student by saying something like "See this? I want you to make one just like this." The teacher then has the student take some objects and make a representation of the array.

(Continued)

Interactive Unit Example with Single-Digit Multiplication (Continued)

IU Descriptor	Single-Digit Multiplication
Display/Identify (i.e., cell 6)	The teacher shows the student a pictorial representation of a four-by-two array. The teacher cues the student by saying something like "See this? Find one here that goes with this." The teacher shows the student three pictorial representations of arrays and has him or her point to the one that is the same as that shown by the teacher.
Display/State (i.e., cell 10)	The teacher shows the student a pictorial representation of a four-by-two array. The teacher cues the student by saying something like "Look at this. What does it show?" The instructor then has the student tell what is shown.
Display/Write (i.e., cell 14)	The teacher shows the student a pictorial representation of a four-by-two array. The teacher cues the student by saying something like "See this? Can you write a number sentence that shows this?" The teacher then has the student write an expression that represents what is shown.
State/Manipulate (i.e., cell 3)	The teacher states the terms of an array by saying something like "Make an array that shows four rows with two items in each row." Then the teacher asks the student to make a representation of the array.
State/Identify (i.e., cell 7)	The teacher states the terms of an array by saying something like "Make an array that shows four rows with two items in each row." The teacher then shows the student three pictorial representations of arrays and asks the student to point to the one that is the same as the one shown by the teacher.
State/State (i.e., cell 11)	The teacher states the terms of an array by saying something like "Listen, tell me about an array that shows four rows with two items in each row." The teacher then has the student restate the input along with the answer.
State/Write (i.e., cell 15)	The teacher states the terms of an array by saying something like "Tell me about an array that shows four rows with two items in each row." The teacher then has the student write an expression to represent the input.
Write/Manipulate (i.e., cell 4)	The teacher shows the student a written expression of a multiplication item. The teacher then asks the student to take some objects and make a representation of the expression in the form of an array.
Write/Identify (i.e., cell 8)	The teacher shows the student a written expression of a multiplication item. The teacher then shows the student three pictorial representations of arrays and asks the student to point to the one that show what is written.
Write/State (i.e., cell 12)	The teacher shows the student a written expression of a multiplication item. The teacher then asks the student to say the expression and the product.
Write/Write (i.e., cell 16)	The instructor shows the student a written expression of a multiplication item. The teacher then asks the student to write (i.e., copy) the expression and the product.

As described earlier in this book, the IU has a multitude of values in the development of selected meanings and principles. Literature sources (Harding, Gust, Goldhawk, & Bierman, 1993; Miller & Mercer, 1993) describe the primary use of alternative representations to be during the acquisition of mathematics principles or skills, little attention is directed toward the use of alternative representations to demonstrate higher-order principles or alternative meanings at the outcome or end stage. Further, the great majority of activities involving alternative representations focus primarily on single-digit combinations. Seldom do we see an illustration such as $23\overline{)276}$ where the student is asked to prepare a manipulative representation of the item and solution. Seldom, also, are we cognizant of the fact that the majority of mathematics used outside of school textbooks results in the development of a product. For example, in nearly every school laboratory activity of physical science, life science, or earth science, mathematics is used to complete a "hands-on" assignment. The mathematics of nearly all vocational-technical education, whether it be cutting a board and joining two pieces at an angle, gapping a plug, or estimating the cost of repairing a fender, is product related. If we examine the various forms of everyday cognition, we note that the mathematics of food purchasing, travel, time, and other daily activities is product related. Thus, there is a very basic need for alternative representations throughout the mathematics educational experiences of the student.

Background for the Operations

Depending on one's perspective, there are a number of factors that should be considered when teaching the operations of arithmetic. Some of these are thought to precede computation per se and others are thought to accompany it. Important considerations for computation are relations, counting, place value, estimation, and expanded notation.

Relations

We stress the importance of students to comprehend and demonstrate their comprehension of basic relationships for numbers. First, as illustrated below, is an understanding of one-to-one correspondence. This is an important relationship that assists students to know about and be able to demonstrate why two different number combinations (e.g., 2 + 4 = ___ and 3 + 3 = ___) provide the same answer (i.e., one-to-one correspondence), as illustrated by an understanding of set membership; set numerosity; and by the matching of the number of items in sets.

Set membership

○ ○ ○ ⟵ ○ ○ ○

○ ○ ○ ○ ○ ○

↓ ↓ ↓ ↓ ↓ ↓

□ □ □ □ □ □

○ ○ ○ ⟵ ○ ○ ○

○ ○ ○ ○ ○ ○

↓ ↓ ↓ ↓ ↓ ↓

□ □ □ □ □ □

Set numerosity

See this representation of 3.

□ □
□

Find another in the following.

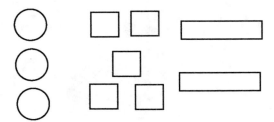

Matching the number of items in sets

See this representation of 3.

Take these materials and make as many representations of 3 as you can.

Look at this representation of 3.

Which of these is a better representation of 3?

Second, the relationships of many-to-one and one-to-many assist the student to grasp the meanings of multiplication and division.

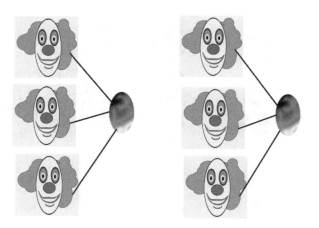

Many to one correspondence: Three clowns share one balloon

Counting

Counting is often considered such a basic skill that it is taken for granted that students can count. Various instructional activities should be designed and implemented to verify that students *can* count. Instruction should also provide students with experience and practice in rote counting.

When teaching counting there are a number of key elements involved. The first is "counting to" or counting to determine the cardinal property of a set. Ginsburg (1989) initiates a discussion of *enumeration* by suggesting that students should (a) know they can count, (b) say the number words in the proper order, (c) count each object in a set and count it only once, and (d) match each number word with an object or set of objects.

When given a set of objects, the students should be able to count to determine the number of objects in the set. Students must be able to determine the cardinal property of one or more sets and state the number in spoken or written language. At some point, they should recognize that they can tell how many items are in a smaller set "by looking." They must also recognize that larger sets, usually with five to seven members or more must be counted.

A second important element is "counting on." Counting on involves the counting of the number of objects in one set and the subsequent counting of the objects in other sets to determine the total number of objects without going back to the first set. For example, you might show a student some objects in one hand and ask him or her to determine the number of objects you have in your hand. You might then close your hand and show some objects in your other hand and ask the student to tell you how many objects are in both hands.

A third important counting behavior is "counting tens." The student should be able to count to ten and group each set of ten. This should be done with 1s to 10s and when appropriate from 10s to 100s and 100s to 1,000s. This should be done with both forward and backward counting activities. In forward counting, the student will determine the number of 10s that can be made from a set of single objects. In backward counting, the student will begin with the set of 10s and determine the numbers of 1s that make the 10s. Activities that focus on one-to-one correspondence, where counting the number of items in two or more groups or counting a number of objects to create a group that has the same number of elements as another group, are also important. Students should also have experience with skip counting (e.g., counting by 2s, 3s, etc.) from different starting points (e.g., count by 3s starting with 2, 11, and so forth). Skip counting is an integral component of relationships that can be described as one-to-many in nature, and it is a natural introduction to multiplication. For example if a teacher shows students four trees with two apples on each tree, the students can count by 2s to determine the number of apples (i.e., $2 + 2 + 2 + 2$, or 4×2). Skip counting as a many-to-one relationship ties in nicely with division (e.g., if given a number of apples and a number of trees, put a specified number of apples on each tree: "Here are six apples. Put two on each tree" (i.e., $2\overline{)6}$).

A Pendulum. Comprehensive counting activities can be undertaken by providing students experiences with tasks such as counting the swings of a pendulum. The pendulum activity enhances students' counting and simultaneously introduces the concepts of *variables, graphing,* and *recording.*

Graphing the Pendulum Swings

Provide 4 strings of different lengths: 6, 12, 18, and 24 inches

Provide 4 blocks of different weights, 1, 2, 3, and 4 ounces

Work with the students to set up a graph

Organize a symbol system for recording weight-by-length data. (i.e., 1 ounce as "+;" 2 ounces as "*;" 3 ounces as "#;" and 4 ounces as "^")

Conduct an experiment by placing different weights on the same length of string.

Count the number of swings for each weight.

Record the data on a chart and graph.

Change the length of string and repeat the process.

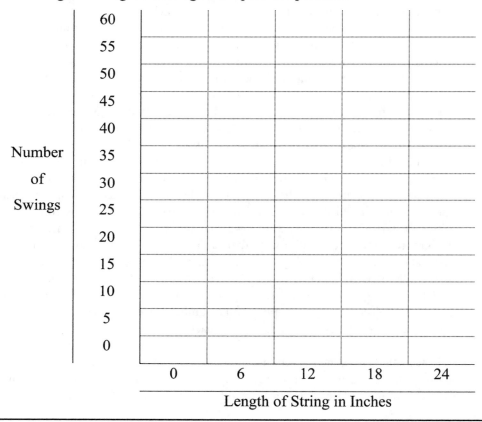

Pendulum activities are designed to involve students in small groups where each member of the group counts the swings independently. When the count has been completed, the students compare their results to ensure that all have the same number of swings. If there are differences, the count should be retaken. When all groups have verified their counts, record their counts on a table and then record the information from the table onto the pendulum graph. This and similar pendulum activities extend the students' experiences in counting by illustrating the processes of tallying, organizing data, and charting.

A Balance Scale. An additional activity that engages the students in active counting is the balance scale count. This activity begins with the teacher displaying a balance scale as illustrated below. The teacher creates the standard of the scale by adding or withdrawing items from one side of the balance scale that is hidden from the students' view. The teacher places a number of objects in the pan that is hidden from students and then asks the students to put a number of objects in their pan to balance the scale. A comparable activity can work in reverse, where the objects are placed on the scale so that it is in balance. The teacher then removes one or more objects on one side of the scale and the students have to remove objects on the other side of the scale in an attempt to get the scale to balance again. This activity provides students with experience in counting as well as addition and subtraction. For addition, the students can identify the total number of items added to their side of the scale to make it balance. For subtraction, the students would have to determine the number of items they would have to remove from their side of the scale to make it balance.

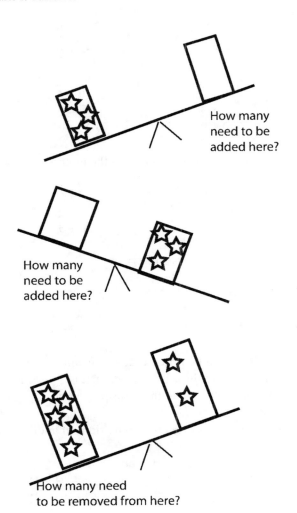

Counting the 10s and Accounting for the 10s. As we have stressed previously, the general emphasis given to counting does not reflect the importance of the process. Moreover, the attention given to *counting the 10s* is highly inadequate. Counting the 10s means that students can count units of 1 and regroup them into units of 10 and thus emphasizes the importance of regrouping. That is, if students have 12 sticks and are asked to count and group the sticks, they will develop one group of 10 and two groups of 1. If students have 74 sticks and are asked to group them, they will develop seven groups of 10 and four groups of 1. If students have 714 sticks and are asked to group them, the students will develop seven groups of 100, one group of 10 and four groups of 1.

Counting the 10s is one of the most essential elements in the foundation of computation. Counting the 10s is fundamental to the (a) utilization and interpretation of alternative representations, (b) development of proficiency in the demonstration and use of alternative algorithms, and (c) the use of expanded notation and the comprehension of place value. The following illustrations highlight the role of counting the 10s.

1. Count and group 26 sticks by 1s to show two 10s and six 1s.
2. Count two 10s and six 1s to show 26. Discuss the similarities between the two illustrations.
3. Represent each of the following as 10s and 1s using expanded notation.

$$\begin{array}{r} 26 \\ +3 \\ \hline 29 \end{array} \qquad \begin{array}{r} 26 \\ -3 \\ \hline 23 \end{array}$$

$$\begin{array}{r} 20 + 6 \\ +3 \\ \hline 20 + 9 \end{array} \qquad \begin{array}{r} 20 + 6 \\ -3 \\ \hline 20 + 3 \end{array}$$

4. Using the materials provided by the teacher, represent each of the following.

$$\begin{array}{r} 20 + 6 \\ +3 \\ \hline 20 + 9 \end{array} \qquad \begin{array}{r} 20 + 6 \\ -3 \\ \hline 20 + 3 \end{array}$$

= 10s and * = 1s

$$\begin{array}{r} \#\# + ****** \\ + *** \\ \hline \#\# + ********* \end{array} \qquad \begin{array}{r} \#\# + ****** \\ - *** \\ \hline \#\# + *** \end{array}$$

It should be noted that all instances of material forms of representations involve expanded notation as illustrated. That is, 37 is the end result of moving through and understanding of 30 + 7 and three 10s plus seven 1s.

5. Examine the following representations of addition and subtraction.

$$\wedge = 100\text{s}, \# = 10\text{s}, \text{ and } * = 1\text{s}$$

$$\begin{array}{r} \wedge\wedge\wedge + \#\# + *** \\ + \wedge\wedge + \# + ** \\ \hline \end{array} \qquad \begin{array}{r} \wedge\wedge\wedge + \#\# + *** \\ - \wedge\wedge + \# + ** \\ \hline \end{array}$$

Write each item as it is shown using numerals.

$$\begin{array}{r} 100, 100, 100 + 10, 10 + 1, 1, 1 \\ + 100, 100 + 10 + 1, 1 \\ \hline \end{array} \qquad \begin{array}{r} 100, 100, 100 + 10, 10 + 1, 1, 1 \\ - 100, 100 + 10 + 1, 1 \\ \hline \end{array}$$

Write each item as it would appear if it was grouped by 100s, 10s, and 1s.

$$300 + 20 + 3 \qquad\qquad 300 + 20 + 3$$
$$\underline{+\ \ 200 + 10 + 2} \qquad\qquad \underline{-\ \ 200 + 10 + 2}$$

Write each item in the traditional format.

$$323 \qquad\qquad 323$$
$$\underline{+\ \ 212} \qquad\qquad \underline{-\ \ 212}$$

The above illustrations display a variety of formats that represent addition and subtraction. They could be presented to students in the sequence shown or in reverse order beginning with the traditional format as a check of their comprehension.

Unusual Combinations of 10s. Illustration A. The teacher can present the students with the following examples and discuss the possibility of conducting addition and subtraction for both right-to-left and left-to-right algorithms.

Left-to-Right		Right-to-Left
$900 +\ \ 0 + 8$		$900 +\ \ 0 + 8$
$\underline{+\ 300 + 60 + 1}$		$\underline{-\ \ 300 + 60 + 1}$
$1{,}200 +\ \ 60 + 9$		600
		$\underline{500 + 40 + 7}$

or

$900 +\ \ 0 + 8$		$900 +\ \ 0 + 8$
$\underline{+\ 300 + 60 + 1}$		$\underline{-\ 300 + 60 + 1}$
9		7
60		40
$1{,}200$		500

Illustration B. The teacher can present the students with a set of problems similar to the ones below and ask them to prepare a manipulative representation of each item using available materials.

$$900 + 20 + 4 \qquad\qquad 900 + 20 + 4$$
$$\underline{+\ \ 400 + 70 + 9} \qquad\qquad \underline{-\ \ 400 + 70 + 9}$$

The students proceed as shown below.

$$\wedge = 100s, \# = 10s, \text{ and } {}^{*} = 1s$$

```
       ∧∧∧∧∧∧∧∧∧ + ## + ****            ∧∧∧∧∧∧∧∧∧ + ## + ****
  +     ∧∧∧∧ + ####### + *********     −   ∧∧∧∧ + ####### + *********
∧∧∧∧∧∧∧∧∧∧∧∧∧ + ######## + *************      ∧∧∧∧ + #### + *****
```

After checking the manipulative representation of the items created by the students, the teacher can then ask them to provide a symbolic representation of their answers.

Place Value

When working with place value it is important that the students recognize that each set of ten items represents one group of 10 and that when we write the 10 we place the digits in a specific sequence. That is, 11 is composed of one "10" and one "1," and the zero in the 10 acts as a place-holder. The students must also be able to conserve the meaning of place value. For example, when given a set of three 10s and four 1s, they should recognize this as 34. If one of the 10s is regrouped to ten 1s the student should still recognize this as 34 even though what is shown is two 10s and fourteen 1s. Students should be able to rename in both directions. They need extended practice in making 56 into five 10s and six 1s, four 10s and sixteen 1s, three 10s and twenty-six 1s, two 10s and thirty-six 1s, and so forth. The same general procedures used with 10s and 1s are also needed with 100s and 1,000s. Students should develop mastery with each increment in place value (e.g., going from 1s to 10s to 100s to 1,000s) as an integral component of any computational routine, and they should be able to describe place value symbolically and in various representations.

Place value is a valuable concept that can be used as a fundamental tool in a number of later mathematical concepts and activities that include:

Estimation
Expanded notation that allows students to use manipulative or pictorial displays to construct meanings
Alternative algorithms
The base ten system with both whole numbers and decimals
Ratio-expressing relationships (e.g., between 10 pennies and 1 dime, or 100 pennies and 1 dollar)
Conservation of a number embedded within alternative representations of the number (e.g., represent 56 in the form of five 10s and six 1s or four 10s and sixteen 1s)
The potential to explain decimal relationships relative to the 1s column
Functions in diagnostics

The primary instructional concerns relative to place value focus on its relationship to the arithmetic operations. This includes debates related to the extent to which place value should be taught directly (e.g., Baroody, 1990; Fuson, 1990; Peterson, Mercer, & O'Shea, 1988) or left to develop intuitively (e.g., Kamii, Lewis, & Livingston, 1993).

Two of the important features of place value are (a) it aids understanding of part-whole relationships and (b) the positions of the digits within a number are related to the base ten property values (e.g., 1s, 10s, . . . ; or 5s, 50s, . . . ; etc.) as they increase by multiples of 10.

Estimation

Estimation, or at a beginning level, "guessing" how many or how much something is, is an important skill to use in computing, evaluating, and monitoring computations. Estimation should be taught and regularly reinforced so that estimating becomes second nature to students, and they come to realize that estimation is more than "guessing." As is the case with adults, students who make estimations of combinations with two or more digits will likely base their estimations on the value of the digit to the farthest left (Lee, 1991). The left-to-right focus of estimations can easily tie in with the left-to-right algorithm in addition, subtraction, or multiplication, which some students may find easier than the right-to-left algorithm.

The concept of estimation can be explored by using items with nonstandard properties, such as estimating whether the amount of water in one jar is the same as in another when the size or structure of the jars is the same or different. This can proceed to estimating the amount of sand in two jars and recognizing that counting would never provide a solution but weighing might. The sand could be changed to marbles and the estimates verified by counting. Different numbers of marbles could be put in the jars and one could determine whether the students truly do estimate by comparing a known (e.g., there are 71 marbles in the jar when it fills up to a specific line) with an unknown (e.g., fill one jar up to a line to represent fewer and another jar up to a line to represent greater). These types of activities with various objects allow students to explore the usefulness of estimation when working with different situations.

Estimation should be integral to all work consisting of two or more digits. In this regard, a typical lesson might begin with two or three examples of items in a lesson where students are asked to estimate the answers to the sample items. For example, if given the following items the student might estimate the answers as 80, 140 or 150, and 50 respectively.

$$54 \qquad\qquad 63 \qquad\qquad 21$$
$$\underline{+\,31} \qquad\qquad \underline{+\,86} \qquad\qquad \underline{+\,33}$$

The students need to recognize estimation as a way to check the answer and then cross-check the actual answer with the estimated answer. Estimation is essential when students use hand-held calculators, as many errors occur when an incorrect digit is inputted.

While estimates represent one general aspect of numeration, counting and other operations confirm the extent to which the estimated number approximated the real number. Activities in this area can include tasks such as counting the number of marbles in a jar or counting the number of different-color marbles in a jar.

Expanded Notation

Expanded notation is highly interrelated with place value and estimation. A form of expanded notation actually links estimation and computation when working with place values of two or more digits. Place value is often reflected in two approaches of expanded notation: set and measurement. The measurement approach uses materials that combine two or more elements. An example would be to arrange a series of individual blocks into rows with a specified number so that some rows are longer than others. Different colors of blocks can also be used to further differentiate the various rows or quantities of blocks. For example, three might be represented by three connected blue blocks and six by six connected green blocks. The difference between the three and six is represented in both the number of blocks connected together and in the use of blocks of different colors. The set approach would use materials of the same shape and size and group them by cardinal representations rather than by length. In this case, three red triangles and six red triangles would be used to create the sets. "Moreness" rather than length would be the basis for comparison. The set approach tends to force regrouping at each 10 and allows for greater diversity in the materials and their arrangements. The items can be spread out or compacted, thereby providing for one-to-one correspondence and conservation of number activities.

The importance of place value can be highlighted with division as well. In the following examples zero is included in the dividend (e.g., $3\,\overline{)1{,}503}$, $3\,\overline{)6{,}015}$, $3\,\overline{)6{,}003}$, $3\,\overline{)4{,}206}$), which requires students to have a complete understanding of place value in order to correctly answer each of the problems. A common response to $3\,\overline{)1{,}503}$ is 51 as the students typically ignore the 0.

Representations of Quantity

Students with difficulties in mathematics must learn that objects and pictures can be used to represent varying mathematical principles and operations, but the operations are actually done symbolically. That is, we can join or separate objects to represent addition or subtraction, but when we add or subtract we do it symbolically with numbers. Assistance in making the transition from objects to symbols with two or more places can be done with expanded notation. For example, when shown the following display of objects to represent 200 + 30 + 3 where there are two 100s, three 10s, and three 1s, it is customary for the teacher to show this as 233.

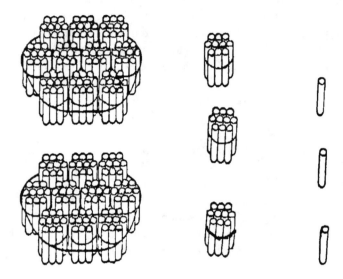

In instances like this, it is common for students to miss the connection between the object and symbolic representations (i.e., the numbers). For this reason, we encourage the use of expanded notation as a transition step.

100	10	1
100	10	1
	10	1

The teacher and students would use a different set of materials and recreate the manipulative/diplay representation of 200 + 30 + 3.

The exchange of items from the manipulative to symbolic and back to the manipulative formats emphasizes the comprehension of the relationship between the manipulative or object representation and the symbolic or numerical format. After much discussion and many illustrations, the teacher could illustrate that 200 + 30 + 3 can be written in a much shorter way as 233, which is equivalent to 200 + 30 + 3. The common form of the number (i.e., 233) can be referred to as the "short way" and 200 + 30 + 3 as the "long way." The teacher could present a variety of number combinations in the short form and ask the students to make manipulative or object representations of the quantities represented. The students should be able to describe 233 as two 100s, three 10s, and three 1s and generalize this to items such as 809 being 800 + 9 and 8,090 as 8,000 + 90.

What is described above is not a recent procedure. The 1849 text *A New System of Arithmetic on an Improved Plan* (Burnham, 1849) urged the use of expanded notation. For example an illustration from addition would be

		Hundreds		*Tens*		*Units*
	252 =	2	+	5	+	2
+	131 =	1	±	3	±	1
	383 =	3	+	8	+	3

Expanded notation provides a framework for interrelating mathematical activities across a wide spectrum. Within this spectrum are activities with denominate numbers such as:

4 yards	5 feet	3 inches
+ 3 yards	4 feet	8 inches
	or	
16 hours	38 minutes	24 seconds
+ 9 hours	46 minutes	14 seconds

CHAPTER SIX

Communicating Mathematics

Communication of mathematics to others and to oneself is an important process capability. The National Council of Teachers of Mathematics standards (NCTM, 2000) suggest four components to communication: (a) organize and consolidate mathematical thinking to communicate with others, (b) express mathematical ideas coherently to others, (c) extend one's own knowledge by incorporating the thinking and strategies of others, and (d) use the language of mathematics precisely. These basic process steps can be extended by using a variety of alternative representations of mathematical ideas (Cawley & Reines, 1996). Among these are the use of manipulatives at both the input and output stages of computation, the use of symbolic formats such as charts and graphs, and the utilization of different forms of written expression.

Students require extensive experience with manipulatives and other representations such as graphs and pictorial displays in order to communicate about and with mathematics. When manipulatives are used as part of the remedial or corrective element in a program, they should always be introduced with something the students already understand and know how to do. Manipulatives should not be used to teach something new unless the students are already familiar and comfortable working with manipulatives in general. If students work with manipulatives to learn a new mathematical concept but are not comfortable with the manipulatives, they might not understand the role or meaning that manipulatives or other forms of representation have in mathematics and may become more confused. It is best to begin use of manipulatives with something the students know and once they have proficiency with the alternative representations, introduce the new meanings or algorithms. The inclusion of a variety of representations provides opportunities for guided discovery and the internalization of mathematical meanings. They provide an alternative to the single rote routine that is characteristic of many approaches.

The present authors prefer the term *manipulatives* to *concrete objects* because the actual use of objects can be extremely meaningful and "abstract." For example, few students are able to use manipulatives to prove that the answer to $3 \div \frac{1}{4}$ is 12 or solve $12\overline{)276}$. When working with numbers, it is important to assist the students in making varying representations in a systematic manner. The students should learn early that numerous forms of communication can take place. One means of conducting alternative representations in a systematic, but flexible format is the Interactive Unit (IU) discussed in chapter 1.

The organization of alternative representations by the Interactive Unit offers an opportunity to systematically build meanings and concepts into a mathematical program. The Interactive Unit also offers an opportunity to focus students' attention and engage them in a variety of activities that focus on proof and elaboration. To illustrate, assume you want to teach $7\overline{)228}$ to students.

The traditional method would approach the problem by saying, "seven into two does not go, so we move over to the next place." What would you do if a student said, "I don't understand. The two stands for two hundred. Are you telling me that seven does not go into two hundred?" Or, "Could you show me this with some materials?" What would the students do if you presented the item and asked, "Can you solve this for me using these sets of toothpicks?"

The Interactive Unit helps to determine whether the problem a student is having with an operation is due to computation errors, the use of inappropriate routines, or conceptual misunderstandings. Let us go back to the example of $7\overline{)228}$ and assume different students did the following with paper-pencil:

$$
\begin{array}{r}
30 \ \text{R8} \\
7\overline{)228} \\
21 \\
\hline
1
\end{array}
\qquad\qquad
\begin{array}{r}
300 \\
7\overline{)228}
\end{array}
$$

$$
\begin{array}{r}
2 \\
30 \ \text{R4} \\
7\overline{)228} \\
210 \\
\hline
18 \\
14 \\
\hline
4
\end{array}
\qquad\qquad
\begin{array}{r}
32 \ \text{R4} \\
7\overline{)228} \\
21 \\
\hline
18 \\
14 \\
\hline
4
\end{array}
$$

A reasonable choice of an instructional scheme would be to have the students create a variety of alternative representations for the item. These might include some of the sixteen combinations of the Interactive Unit. Let us assume the instructor presented the students with $7\overline{)228}$ in a written format and asked the students to "make it." The representation would look something like this:

Step 1: 1111111)##$$11111111

Step 2: 1111111)$$11111111

Key:
\# = 100's
\$ = 10's
1 = 1's

$$$$$$$$$$

$$$$$$$$$$

3

Step 3: 1111111)$$11111111

$$$$$$$$$$

$$$$$$$$$$

3

Step 4: 1111111)$11111111

3   2

Step 5: 1111111)11111111

11111111111

3   2   R4

Step 6: 1111111)1111

The key for 100s, 10s, and 1s really means you are showing the student objects such as popsicle sticks grouped in 100s and 10s.

The question posed to the students is, "How many sets with this many [1111111] can you make here [##]?" The answer is "none" because there are only two 100s and you need seven to make a set [step 1]. We then regroup the two 100s into two sets of 10 each and the total number of 10s becomes twenty-two [step 2]. We can now ask the question, "How many sets with this many [1111111] can you make here [$$$$$$$$$$$$$$$$$$$$$$]?" The students can group the sets into three sets of 7 [step 3], with one set remaining [step 4]. The students can regroup the remaining set of 10 into 1s which results in eighteen 1s that they can then make into two sets of 7 each [step 5] with a remainder of 4 [step 6]. Notice that the division has been completed without any multiplication or subtraction. All that was truly needed was an ability to count and an understanding of place value. Notice also, that the students were not misled by being told that 7 does not go into 2 [200].

The role of the Interactive Unit is not to provide rote, or drill and practice, exercises or to provide concrete experiences. The role of the Interactive Unit is to provide opportunities for students to communicate mathematics and demonstrate, prove, and justify their approaches with alternative representations.

There is an important role in computation for explicitness, modeling, and practice. The uses of alternative representations in the Interactive Unit are quite explicit. With manipulatives, for example, we say, "Watch me. Do what I do." and set forth a model for the students to follow. The students are encouraged to make numerous representations and demonstrate an increase in speed in doing so. Numerous instances of practice are provided with the range of interactions so the students experience the interrelationships among the various representations. When students make the transition to written symbols, they are better able to understand what is being symbolized and that the algorithm is a symbolized way of representing a mathematical relationship.

Alternative representations involve students as individuals and as group members. When working as individuals, the students communicate to themselves in varying ways through the act of *pondering*. For the students who are aware and competent in using alternative representations, pondering allows students to represent different forms and degrees of mathematics to the self. For the students in a group, the general process involves *brainstorming*, where students display and share different ideas and formats. The group mechanism allows students to critique, ask questions, clarify, and improve upon their ideas and understanding of concepts and demonstrations of concepts.

One important set of activities that assist students to communicate mathematically is rooted in establishing *connections* (Cawley & Foley, 2002; House & Coxford, 1995). Connections focus on the uses and applications of mathematics principles and skills in other content areas or real-life situations. An example of this might be an analysis of temperature reading over the course of a week or month. The skills involved could include counting, tallying, adding, dividing, charting or graphing, and reporting.

Knowing about and Doing Arithmetic

What do we want to know about arithmetic, and what do we want to be able to do in arithmetic? Some of the things we want to know and be able to do with arithmetic computation are listed separately for each operation, and there are basic prerequisites for all the operations.

Spoken/written number symbols (e.g., "three" = "xxx" versus "3" = "xxx")
Counting by 1s
Skip counting
One-to-one correspondence
One-to-many relationships
Many-to-one relationships
Simple regrouping and renaming

Memorization of Basic Facts

After the students have reached an understanding of what to know about an operation and have learned about doing an operation, it is time to work with them to develop strategies for memorizing the basic facts and other components of the operation. The procedure described below is applicable to all four operations. Here we use the example of addition, and we refer to this procedure as "A + H."

The student is presented with a simulated set of addition facts in which letters replace numerals. The student is asked to examine the four simulated facts and to remember them utilizing any method he or she wishes. The teacher can make suggestions, such as writing them down, saying them to oneself, or working with another student who might read them and the target student recite them back. For addition, the facts are:

$$\begin{array}{cccc} A & D & L & M \\ +H & +Z & +B & +C \\ \hline P & T & E & G \end{array}$$

The students are made aware that when they finish the memory task, there will be a test. The students are given as much time as needed and any materials such as a pencil and paper they might need. Upon completion of the memory task, the teacher engages the students in a discussion that focuses upon the method the students utilized to remember the simulated combinations. It is the method of the individual that is important, and what the teacher should do is to make suggestions as to how to make the method more efficient and effective. The teacher should not criticize the method except to compare it with other methods.

The test for addition is shown below.

$$\begin{array}{llll} 1)\ \ A & 2)\ \ H & 3)\ \ Z & 4)\ \ L \\ \ \ \ +H & \ \ \ +A & \ \ \ +D & \ \ \ +B \end{array}$$

$$\begin{array}{llll} 5)\ \ E & 6)\ \ G & 7)\ \ D & 8)\ \ D \\ \ \ \ -B & \ \ \ -C & \ \ \ +B & \ \ \ +Z \end{array}$$

$$\begin{array}{lll} 9)\ \ A & 10)\ \ B & 11)\ \ T \\ \ \ \ +P & \ \ \ \ +L & \ \ \ \ -Z \end{array}$$

The test has eleven items. The initial item, $A + H$ provides an element of familiarity to the student, as it is a direct representation of a memorized item; items, $H + A$, $Z + D$, and $B + L$ represent the commutative property of addition; $E - B$, $G - C$, and $T - Z$ represent the interrelationships between addition and subtraction; and $D + B$ and $A + P$ are distractors, which the students are not able to complete due to a lack of meaning. The key features of this task are to determine (a) the strategy used by the students to memorize to combinations, (b) what, if anything, the students did to store the information until it was time to take the test, (c) how the students went about taking the test, and (d) how the students managed the distractors.

Paired-associate memory tasks such as these are best conducted with a limited number of combinations (we generally use four items), by allowing the student as much time or as many repetitions as desired, and by allowing the student to use a method that is familiar.

Addition

Things to Know about Addition

Addition is a process that joins two or more disjoint sets so that all members of each set are represented by a common element (i.e., the sum). The resulting sum can be compared with other sums. A sum can be obtained by using the following arithmetic principles.

The addition of a number other than zero results in a different number: You have 7. What do you have to add to 7 to make 7 greater than 8?

Commutative property: Why do 2 + 3 and 3 + 2 make 5?

Associative property: Why do (3 + 2) + 1 and 3 + (2 + 1) have the same answer?

Equivalence: One number is 4. Another number is 5. What do you have to do to the 4 to make it the same as 5?

> One set has 4 lions. Another set has 4 tigers. When asked to count the lions and tigers the students may say there are 4. If asked, "Can you show me why do both sets have the same number?" How might the students respond?

Add to greater: You have 4. You want to make it a greater number. What do you have to do?

Subtract to greater: You have 4 and 6. You want to change the 6 so the 4 will be greater. What do you have to do?

Add to fewer: You have a 4 and a 7. What can you add to the 4 so that it will be greater than 4, but fewer than 7?

Subtract to fewer: You have a 4 and a 7. You want to change the 7 so that it will be fewer than the 4. What can you do?

Conservation: 111111 = 6 = 1   1   1   1   1   1 = ? Why?

Class inclusion: You have 3 brown marbles and 2 white marbles. Do you have more brown marbles than marbles? Or: You have 3 brown marbles and 2 white marbles. How many white marbles do you need so that you will have more white marbles than marbles? Help the students to understand that you cannot have more brown or white marbles than marbles.

Reversibility and interchangeability: Ask the students to examine the following two items and explain how the same numbers can be used to make these different combinations.

$$4 + 2 = \underline{\quad}; 2 + 4 = \underline{\quad}; 6 - 4 = \underline{\quad}; 6 - 2 = \underline{\quad}$$
$$4 + \underline{\quad} = 6; \underline{\quad} + 2 = \underline{\quad}; 6 - \underline{\quad} = 2; 6 - \underline{\quad} = 4$$

Sensibility: 21 = two 10s and one 1; 12 = one 10 and two 1s. Why do these two items make sense?

Why does the following make sense?

$$\begin{array}{r} 21 \\ + 12 \\ \hline 33 \end{array}$$

Why does the following not make sense?

$$\begin{array}{r} 21 \\ + 12 \\ \hline 83 \end{array}$$

Classification: Pears and apples = fruit   Why do 3 pears and 2 apples = 5 fruits

Boys and girls = students   Why do 5 boys and 3 girls make 8 students?

One-to-one correspondence:

> Why do 1 + 5, 2 + 4, and 3 + 3 each make 6?
>
> Why is 4 + 3 ≠ 6?
>
> You have 6. What do you need to do to make it 9?
>
> You have 9. What do you have to do to make 6?
>
> You have 6. What do you have to do to make none?
>
> You have 0 (none). What do you have to do to make 6?
>
> If you are given XXXXXX; what do you have to do to get XXXXXXX?
>
> What comes next in the sequence? XX   XXXX   XXXXXX   ?
>
> What number did you add to make the sequence?

Make each of the following correct:

$$\begin{array}{r} 3 \\ +\ 4 \\ \hline 8 \end{array} \qquad \begin{array}{r} 5 \\ +\ 1 \\ \hline 5 \end{array} \qquad \begin{array}{r} 2 \\ +\ 3 \\ \hline 4 \end{array}$$

Which one of the following is incorrect? Why?

$$\begin{array}{r} 4 \\ +\ 2 \\ \hline 6 \end{array} \qquad \begin{array}{r} 3 \\ +\ 2 \\ \hline 6 \end{array}$$

Why are both of the following correct?

$$\begin{array}{r} 6 \\ +\ 3 \\ \hline 9 \end{array} \qquad 6 + 3 = 9$$

Why is one of the following correct and the other incorrect?

$$\begin{array}{r} 6 \\ +\ 3 \\ \hline 8 \end{array} \qquad 6 + 3 = 9$$

or

$$\begin{array}{r} 6 \\ +\ 3 \\ \hline 9 \end{array} \qquad 6 + 3 = 8$$

Make the following correct

$$\begin{array}{r} 5 \\ +\ 1 \\ \hline 7 \end{array}$$

Fill in the empty spaces. Why are the answers to all the items the same?

$$\begin{array}{r} 5 \\ +\ 3 \\ \hline 8 \end{array} \qquad \begin{array}{r} 5 \\ +\ \underline{} \\ \hline 8 \end{array} \qquad \begin{array}{r} 6 \\ +\ \underline{} \\ \hline 8 \end{array}$$

Additive identity: When zero is added to a number, the number does not change. Zero is a place value holder in items comprised of two or more digits.

$$8 + 0 = \underline{} \qquad 9 + 0 = \underline{} \qquad \begin{array}{r} 203 \\ +\ 140 \\ \hline \end{array}$$

One: When one is added to a number, the answer is the next number.

$$7 + 1 = \underline{} \qquad 8 + 1 = \underline{}$$

Things to Know When Doing Addition

It is common to begin single-digit addition with the lower number and for items with two or more digits to begin with the right lower digit.

Addition involves joining only two numbers at any one time.

$$
\begin{array}{r}
23 \\
31 \\
+\ 22 \\
\end{array}
\quad 2 + 1 = 3 \text{ is illustrative of this principle.}
$$

Addition involves the temporary storage of the sum of two numbers in order to add a third number.

$$
\begin{array}{r}
23 \\
31 \\
+\ 22 \\
\end{array}
\quad
\begin{array}{l}
2 + 1 = 3, \text{ three is held in temporary storage} \\
\text{and recombined to } 3 + 3.
\end{array}
$$

Numerous multidigit numbers can be joined in any sequence to represent the commutative and associative properties.

$$
\begin{array}{r}
3,455 \\
2,132 \\
+\ 4,212 \\
\end{array}
$$

Addition may take place from any place value setting.

$$
\begin{array}{r}
24 \\
+\ 13 \\
7 \\
+\ 30 \\
\hline
37 \\
\end{array}
\qquad
\begin{array}{r}
24 \\
+\ 13 \\
30 \\
+\ 7 \\
\hline
37 \\
\end{array}
\qquad
\begin{array}{r}
3,455 \\
2,132 \\
+\ 4,212 \\
700 \\
90 \\
9,000 \\
+\quad 9 \\
\hline
9,799 \\
\end{array}
$$

In addition renaming/regrouping is generally a right to left sequence, although the students may go from left to right.

$$
\begin{array}{r}
236 \\
+\ 886 \\
\hline
\end{array}
\quad
\begin{array}{r}
236 \\
+\ 886 \\
\hline
\end{array}
$$

becomes   becomes

$$
\begin{array}{r}
11 \\
236 \\
+\ 886 \\
\hline
1122 \\
\end{array}
\qquad
\begin{array}{r}
236 \\
+\ 886 \\
10 \\
11 \\
+\ 12 \\
\hline
1122 \\
\end{array}
$$

Renaming/regrouping is meaningful, as it is interpreted with place value. The first two examples below show two methods in which the students do not utilize a "carrying" notation and the third shows the traditional algorithm that does utilize the "carrying" notation.

```
   236          236           11
 + 886        + 886          236
  1000           12        + 886
   110          110         1122
 +  12        + 1000
  1122         1122
```

Subtraction

Things to Know about Subtraction

Subtraction is *difference*; it is not "take away." The reason there is a difference between two numbers is that the sets of numbers lack *one-to-one* correspondence. When the numbers in each set are the same, there is one-to-one correspondence and if there is no difference, the answer is 0. The difference principle is evident when students analyze and discuss situations similar to the following:

Determinations of what number must be added to another to make them the same, as in the following example.

Hector has 4 apples in his pail. Lucy has 2 apples in her pail. How many apples must Lucy add to her pail so she will have as many apples as Hector?

How much larger/smaller one number is than another as shown in the following examples.

Jamel has 4 apples in his pail. Nelson has 2 apples in his pail. How many more apples does Jamel have than Nelson?

Jamel has 4 apples in his pail. Nelson has 2 apples in his pail. How many fewer apples does Nelson have in his pail than Jamel?

What remains of a quantity after part of it has been removed.

Marques has 4 apples in his pail. Tara has 2 apples in her pail. If Marques put 2 of his apples in Tara's pail, how many apples would be in Marques's pail?

Marques has 4 apples in his pail. Tara has 2 apples in her pail. If Tara put 2 of her apples in Marques's pail, how many apples would Tara have in her pail?

Subtraction takes place in only one column, whether the column is the 1s, 10s, 100s, etcetera, and the largest digit in the minuend that requires renaming is 8 when the subtrahend is 9 (i.e., $18 - 9$; $180 - 90$ require renaming). Thus, understanding place value is fundamental to subtraction involving two or more digits.

There are many approaches to subtraction. Students can learn the traditional decomposition method, borrow-payback, the complementary, and/or the additive method (Reisman, 1977). They can also learn multiple ways of completing items such as going from right-to-left or left-to-right. They can integrate and compare various item formats such as manipulative representations, expanded notation, and the traditional numeration format.

Addition and subtraction are inverse operations. Addition and subtraction should be taught simultaneously. Students should know that addition can be proved by subtraction (e.g., $6 + 2 + 5 = 13$ as $13 - 5 = \_\_\_ - 2 = \_\_\_ - 6 = 0$) and subtraction can be proved by addition (e.g., $13 - 6 = 7$ as $6 + \_\_\_ = 13$). To illustrate the first principle, assume that a teacher presented the students with the following and asked them to explain why the answer is the same for each item. The students should reply with something like, "It's because the difference (i.e., 5) between the two numbers is the same." The teacher might extend the query by asking, "Can you show me how this happens?" The students could refer to the second principle and demonstrate the one-to-one correspondence in the different answers.

$$
\begin{array}{r} 8 \\ -3 \\ \hline 5 \end{array}
\qquad
\begin{array}{r} 9 \\ -4 \\ \hline 5 \end{array}
\qquad
\begin{array}{r} 6 \\ -1 \\ \hline 5 \end{array}
$$

The teacher could create an addition item and ask the same question, "Why are the answers the same?" and the students could respond with something similar to: "They are all the same because the numbers in each item are in one-to-one correspondence."

$$
\begin{array}{r} 5 \\ +3 \\ \hline 8 \end{array}
\qquad
\begin{array}{r} 4 \\ +4 \\ \hline 8 \end{array}
\qquad
\begin{array}{r} 6 \\ -2 \\ \hline 8 \end{array}
$$

Assume further that the teacher presents the students with the following items and asks them to explain why the answer to each item is 0. The students would be expected to indicate that either (a) the number of items in each set is the same, so there is no difference or (b) the number of items in each set are in one-to-one correspondence so they are the same.

$$
\begin{array}{r} 8 \\ -8 \\ \hline 0 \end{array}
\qquad
\begin{array}{r} 7 \\ +7 \\ \hline 0 \end{array}
\qquad
\begin{array}{r} 3 \\ -3 \\ \hline 0 \end{array}
$$

Things to Know When Doing Subtraction

Single-digit subtraction involves finding the difference between a larger number (e.g., 8) and a smaller number (e.g., 5). This is an important principle of subtraction because it reduces the chance that a "bug" will occur (Baroody, 1990). Experience with missing addends is important as students complete activities such as ___ + 5 = 8 where the greater number is the "bottom" or second number. It is important when students encounter word problems such as the following, where the smaller number is presented first:

> Albie has 5 apples. Marie has 9 apples. How many apples does Albie need to have as many apples as Marie?

Student use of "facts" should be accurate and rapid (NCTM, 2000). Students' knowledge of the facts should be accompanied by a capability to generate responses to unknowns (Putnam, DeBettencourt, & Leinhardt, 1990).

Using Multiple Algorithms. When subtraction involves two or more digits, the students should be able to use multiple algorithms. Doing a single item using three different algorithms can represent a higher quality of mathematics than doing three different items using the same algorithm.

Expanded Notation. Students should be able to represent subtraction of two or more digits using expanded notation. They should be able to use expanded notation to explain the transition from manipulative to symbolic representations.

Interrelationships between Addition and Subtraction. Use the addition/subtraction table below to answer the following questions.

What is the number sequence in row 1?
What is the number sequence in column 1?
In what way are the number sequences in row 1 and column 1 similar or different?
What is the number sequence in row 4?
What is the number sequence in row 5?
In what way are the number sequences in rows 4 and 5 similar or different?
What is the number sequence in row 3?
What is the number sequence in column 5?
In what way are the number sequences in row 3 and column 5 similar or different?
Locate the row and column that represent 10 − 2.
Locate the row and the column that represent 5 + 5.
Locate the rows and the columns that represent 5 + 9 is greater than 4 + 5.
Locate the rows and the columns that represent 8 − 2 is greater than 5 − 1.

+,−	1	2	3	4	5	6	7	8	9
1	2	3	4	5	6	7	8	9	10
2	3	4	5	6	7	8	9	10	11
3	4	5	6	7	8	9	10	11	12
4	5	6	7	8	9	10	11	12	13
5	6	7	8	9	10	11	12	13	14
6	7	8	9	10	11	12	13	14	15
7	8	9	10	11	12	13	14	15	16
8	9	10	11	12	13	14	15	16	17
9	10	11	12	13	14	15	16	17	18

Finding Missing Numbers. This activity extends the students' understanding of the relationship between addition and subtraction. The task presents the students with an addition and subtraction facts table and asks them to fill in the missing values. The teacher could take any table and delete selected combinations as desired.

+,−	1	2	?	4	5	6	7	?	9
1	2	3	4	?	6	7	8	9	10
?	3	?	5	6	7	8	9	10	11
3	4	5	?	7	8	9	?	11	?
?	5	6	7	8	9	10	?	12	13
5	?	7	8	9	?	11	12	?	14
6	7	8	9	10	?	12	13	14	?
7	8	?	10	11	12	?	14	15	16
8	9	10	11	?	13	14	15	16	17
9	?	?	12	13	14	15	16	17	18

YAP and YAN

YAP and YAN are two activities that provide students with an opportunity to examine the interrelationships between addition and subtraction, YAP, and between multiplication and division,

YAN. YAP provides the students with a standard in which YAP is 4 as illustrated by the four dots. This is accompanied by a set of number sentences composed of nonwords. The task for the student is to determine the value of each of the nonword expressions and to then write these as number sentences using numerals.

$$YAP : :$$

HIF + HIF = YAP   _____ + _____ = _____

ZIM – HIF = YAP   _____ – _____ = _____

ZIM + HIF = CIM   _____ + _____ = _____

HIF – HIF = TIB   _____ – _____ = _____

TIS + TIS = ZIM   _____ + _____ = _____

ZIM + TIS = ARB   _____ + _____ = _____

ARB – HIF = DOF   _____ – _____ = _____

DOF – HIF = WUM   _____ – _____ = _____

WUM – YAP = LEB   _____ – _____ = _____

DOF + TIS = BAZ   _____ + _____ = _____

When finished, the students are instructed to complete the following chart:

0 = _____   6 = _____

1 = _____   7 = _____

3 = _____   8 = _____

4 = _____   9 = _____

5 = _____   10 = _____

Upon completion of the chart, the students are provided with items similar to the following:

YAP	TIS	BAZ	WUM
+ TIS	– LEB	– ARB	+ HIF

A review of the completed items takes place and then a discussion as to the meaning of the number words and how the names given to the numerals are arbitrary. The true meaning is in the cardinal property associated with the "names."

Multiplication

Things to Know about Multiplication

Multiplication expresses the number obtained when joining disjoint sets where each set has the same cardinal number (e.g., 6 sets each with 2 items per set).

Multiplication can be represented by a many-to-one relationship among or between sets as illustrated below:

Look at the clowns. From the choices below, point to the picture that shows how many balloons the last set of clowns should have. [Answer: C]

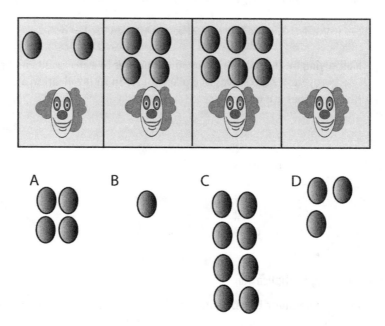

Commutative Property. The numbers can be multiplied in any order. This reflects the abstract nature of numerals; however, in applied situations 6 packages of shoes, with 2 shoes in each package means $6 \times 2 = 12$ but not $2 \times 6 = 12$.

Associative Property. When three or more numbers are to be multiplied, two numbers must be multiplied first, and then the product of the two numbers is multiplied by the third number and so on.

$$2 \times 3 \times 4 = ?$$
$$(2 \times 3) \times 4 = 6 \times 4 = 24$$
$$2 \times (3 \times 4) = 2 \times 12 = 24$$
$$3 \times 2 \times 4 \times 5 = ?$$
$$(3 \times 2) \times 4 \times 5 = (6 \times 4) \times 5 = 24 \times 5 = 120$$
$$3 \times (2 \times 4) \times 5 = (3 \times 8) \times 5 = 24 \times 5 = 120$$
$$3 \times 2 \times (4 \times 5) = 3 \times (2 \times 20) = 3 \times 40 = 120$$

Distributive Property for Multiplication over Addition. To multiply a number by a sum of two numbers you can add first and then multiply or multiply first and then add.

$$4 \times (2 + 3) = ?$$
$$4 \times (2 + 3) = 4 \times 5 = 20$$
$$(4 \times 2) + (4 \times 3) = 8 + 12 = 20$$

Even or odd numbers can be multiplied to yield even or odd products:

Any number multiplied by an even number is an even product (e.g., $2 \times 4 = 8, 6 \times 6 = 36, 6 \times 7 = 42$, etc.)

An odd number multiplied by an odd number is an odd product (e.g., $5 \times 7 = 35, 7 \times 3 = 21$, etc.)

Multiplicative Identity Property. Any number multiplied by 1 is that number:

$$7 \times 1 = 7, 72 \times 1 = 72, 121 \times 1 = 121, 465 \times 1 = 465$$

Multiplying by Zero. Multiplying any number by zero results in a product of zero (e.g., $8 \times 0 = 0$, $0 \times 4 = 0$, etc.). Zero serves as a placeholder in multiplication and is used to store place value and numbers that are renamed:

```
   309            3,069
   ×2              ×2
 becomes         becomes
   1               11
   309            3,069
   ×2              ×2
 6 1 8          6, 1 3 8
```

Things to Know When Doing Multiplication

Alternative Algorithms. Students should know that there are many ways to do multiplication (Morrow, 1998). For example, left-to-right:

```
   324
   ×2
   600
    40
 +   8
   648
```

When multiplying with multidigit numbers, the students can begin in any place value position.

```
   324                        324
   ×2                         ×6
    40  (20×2)                120  (20×6)
   600  (300×2)             1,800  (300×6)
 +   8  (4×2)              +   24  (4×6)
   648                      1,944
```

Various representations or formats can be used as well:

$$
\begin{array}{r}
324 \\
\times\, 12 \\
\hline
\end{array}
\qquad \text{as} \qquad
\begin{array}{r}
12 \times 324 \\
3{,}600 \\
240 \\
+\quad 48 \\
\hline
3{,}888
\end{array}
$$

or

$$
\begin{array}{r}
386 \\
\times\, 12 \\
\hline
\end{array}
\qquad \text{as} \qquad
\begin{array}{r}
12 \times 386 \\
3{,}600 \\
960 \\
+\quad 72 \\
\hline
4{,}632
\end{array}
$$

Students should be alert to the implications of place value in any multiplication beyond single digits.

Relationships between and among Sets. Present students with the following and ask them to describe and demonstrate why three such different number combinations have the same answer or why three different number combinations have different answers.

$$
\begin{array}{ccc}
6 & 9 & 12 \\
\times\,6 & \times\,4 & \times\,3 \\
\hline
36 & 36 & 36
\end{array}
$$

or

$$
\begin{array}{ccc}
6 & 9 & 12 \\
\times\,4 & \times\,5 & \times\,6 \\
\hline
24 & 45 & 72
\end{array}
$$

Present the students with the following and ask them to explain and demonstrate why three numbers multiplied by one have different answers.

$$
\begin{array}{ccc}
6 & 9 & 12 \\
\times\,1 & \times\,1 & \times\,1 \\
\hline
6 & 9 & 12
\end{array}
$$

Mastery and Automaticity. As students develop a variety of ways of knowing about multiplication, mastery of the basic facts should be stressed. Memorization of the multiplication "facts" or "tables" can be presented such that there are only three "tables" that need to be memorized. Provide a demonstration of multiplication with an array similar to the following example.

In the table below, column A shows 5×6 or 5 rows and 6 items in each row. Reorganize the rows to show 2 rows of 6 and 3 rows of 6 as shown in column B. Discuss the similarities and differences in the two representations (i.e., columns A and B). Reorganize the array again to show 1 row of 6 and 4 rows of 6 as in column C. Assist the students to know that the rows and columns of the array can be reorganized in many different ways. Extend this to other arrays such as 8×4, and so on.

A	B	C
xxxxx	xxxxx	xxxxx
xxxxx	xxxxx	
xxxxx		xxxxx
xxxxx	xxxxx	xxxxx
xxxxx	xxxxx	xxxxx
	xxxxx	xxxxx

As the students learn the relationships among the rows and columns, suggest that different combinations can be used to represent the same product.

5×6 can be written as $2 \times 6 + 3 \times 6$ or $1 \times 6 + 4 \times 6$
8×4 can be written as $2 \times 4 + 6 \times 4$, $1 \times 4 + 7 \times 4$, or $3 \times 4 + 5 \times 4$, etc.

Ask the student to explain why items such as $2 \times 4 + 6 \times 4$ are equal to 8×4.

Using the above activities as an introduction, indicate to the students that you know an interesting way to do multiplication that minimizes the amount of facts they have to "memorize." Tell the students there are initially only three sets of "facts" or three "tables" to remember. They are the 2s, 5s, and 10s. Begin with 5×5 and prepare an array to represent 5×5. Restructure the array into a 2×5 and a 3×5 representation. Tell the students that if they know the 2s and the 5s tables, they can figure out the 3s tables without having to memorize them. Guide them through the process that $5 \times 5 - 2 \times 5$ is 3×5 and given that they know the 5s, they know that $3 \times 5 = 15$. Ask them if they can figure out 7×5 if they know the 2s and 5s tables. Extract the process of $5 \times 5 + 2 \times 5$ as 7 times 5 and represent this as an array if necessary to show that 2×5 and 5×5 is equal to 7×5. Continue with items such as 8×6 and call attention to knowing the 10s and 2s tables. Suggest that $10 \times 6 - 2 \times 6 = 8 \times 6$; where $10 \times 6 = 60$ and $2 \times 6 = 12$; so $60 - 12 = 48$.

Suggest a discussion about selected principles of multiplication such as:

Role of zero
Role of 1

Division

Things to Know about Division

Determining the number of sets, with each set having the same number
Many-to-one correspondence
Missing factor
Partitioning or measurement
Ratio
Division by 1
Division by 0
Remainder, as an integer or repeating decimal
Division as a left-to-right operation
Alternative representations for division
Alternative algorithms for division
Formats for division

$2\overline{)4}$ $\qquad$ $4 \div 2$ $\qquad$ $\frac{4}{2}$

Higher-order outcomes for division would be attained when the students can demonstrate division as:

a many-to-one relationship
equivalence in groups or group size
interchanges between *partitioning* and *measurement ratio*

Basic understandings of division can be introduced long before computation with division is taught.

Things to Know When Doing Division

Single-Digit Division. Single-digit division provides numerous opportunities for students to interact with the process of division and explore a variety of features. For example, we can show the students one or two exemplars and ask them to create as many items as they can that are similar to the exemplars provided (e.g., $4\overline{)8}$, $3\overline{)9}$, etc.). The general model of creative thinking can be used to score items developed by students. (i.e., (a) frequency, or number of items produced, (b) divergence, or the number of different items created, and (c) originality, or the number of items that are unique compared to items created by other students).

Evaluative Thinking. The students can engage in the process of evaluative thinking, which requires analysis and judgment as to which members of a group are "better" than others. For example if they are given, $4\overline{)8}$, $5\overline{)10}$, and $3\overline{)6}$, students are asked to select the one that in their opinion is a better representation of division. There is no one correct response, except in relation to the one the students choose in contrast to another.

Activities for Learning Division Students can be asked to contrast varying number combinations. For example, given $2\overline{)4}$, $4\overline{)8}$, and $6\overline{)12}$, ask the students to explain why all three items have the same answer. Or, students can be asked to explain why $3\overline{)6}$, $5\overline{)15}$, and $4\overline{)24}$, have different answers.

Students can be presented with items similar to the following and asked to complete each item [24 ÷ ___ = ___ ÷ ___ = ___]. A number of students can be asked to put the items on the chalkboard for review. Each student is likely to have problems with different combinations, which will serve as a basis for discussion about the variability among the problems created by the students.

The students can be presented with sequencing tasks and asked to complete or extend the sequence as illustrated (e.g., $2\overline{)4}$, $3\overline{)6}$, $4\overline{)8}$, ___, ___).

Show the students the problem $4\overline{)8}$ and ask them to make a representation of the problem using the set of blocks they are given.

The students can be shown the following and asked to explain how each represents division.

$$4\overline{)8} \qquad\qquad 8 \div 4 \qquad\qquad \tfrac{8}{4}$$

The students can be shown the following and asked to explain how it is that the numbers that are multiplied in each example are only two times as big as each other, yet the answer to the second problem is four times as big as the other. And, for division, why does dividing a number that is four times as big as another number that is being divided result in an answer that is only two times as big as the other answer?

$$3 \times 4 = 12 \qquad 6 \times 8 = 48$$

or

$$3\overline{)12}^{\,4} \qquad 6\overline{)48}^{\,8}$$

There are actually many more activities that can be utilized with single-digit combinations to build conceptualizations and skills with division. Shifting from single-digit divisors to multidigit divisors requires a distinct set of prerequisite skills. Among them are:

Counting by 10s, both backward and forward
Place value
Expanded notation
Estimation
Knowledge that division is a left-to-right operation

Interrelationships between Multiplication and Division. Use the multiplication/division table below to answer the following questions.

What is the number sequence in row 1?
What is the number sequence in column 1?
In what way are the number sequences in row 1 and column 1 similar or different?
What is the number sequence in row 4?
What is the number sequence in row 5?
In what way are the number sequences in row 4 and row 5 similar or different?
What is the number sequence in row 3?
What is the number sequence in column 5?
In what way are the number sequences in row 3 and column 5 similar or different?
Locate the row and column combination that would show you $4\overline{)16}$.
Locate the row and column combination that would show you 4×8.
Locate the combinations of rows and columns that would show you that 5×9 is greater than 4×5.
Locate the rows and columns that represent that $6\overline{)54}$ is greater than $8\overline{)24}$.

×, ÷	1	2	3	4	5	6	7	8	9
1	1	2	3	4	5	6	7	8	9
2	2	4	6	8	10	12	14	16	18
3	3	6	9	12	15	18	21	24	27
4	4	8	12	16	20	24	28	32	36
5	5	10	15	20	25	30	35	40	45
6	6	12	18	24	30	36	42	48	54
7	7	14	21	28	35	42	49	56	63
8	8	16	24	32	40	48	56	64	72
9	9	18	27	36	45	54	63	72	81

CHAPTER SEVEN

Teaching the Operations Using Whole Numbers

Teaching the arithmetic operations involves a series of choices among curricula, tasks, and instructional philosophies. Throughout this book we have advocated for a defined curriculum in which the sequence of items is sufficiently detailed to enable the teacher to closely monitor an individual or group of students and make decisions based on the students' performance. We also support the utilization of a variety of tasks for each item in the curriculum. Moreover, the district, school, or teacher should use an instructional philosophy that is aligned with what and how content is taught. It is also important to recognize that the instructional philosophy might change in specific instances or for specific goals.

The choice of an instructional philosophy will often be guided by the outcomes expected by the teacher, school, or district. For example, if it is the goal of the district, school, or teacher that students should be competent problem solvers, then one should consider the use of an instructional philosophy that has a problem-solving focus. This might place the teacher in the role of a "problem poser," who uses probes, strategies, and queries to guide students in the learning process. If the goals of the district are more focused on outcomes where students learn and apply mathematics skills in real-life situations or in situations connected to other subjects and topics, then instruction should place the students in those types of situations to both learn and apply mathematics. If, on the other had, the goal is that the students develop competence in the basic skills of arithmetic and problem solving, then the instruction should be designed to elicit that type of outcome. Overall, there should be an alignment among the philosophy, goals, and outcomes that influences how instruction is implemented.

An important distinction in teaching the arithmetic operations with whole numbers is between developmental and remedial efforts. Developmental efforts imply that the students will be taught something for the first time or at a time when they have only had a limited amount of time or experience to achieve mastery. An example of developmental instruction might be teaching two-digit subtraction to students who are eight years old and in the second grade. Remedial efforts imply correction of inappropriate or incomplete knowledge and meanings and the inappropriate use of routines. An example of this might be teaching two-digit subtraction to students who are fourteen years old.

In each case, the students might subtract the smaller digit from the larger digit (e.g., 90 −27, subtract the zero from the 7 and the 2 from the 9). For the younger students, the use of this algorithm might be considered part of the development and inventive processes they are experiencing. But for the older students this is likely to represent a serious distortion of both their conceptualization of subtraction and understanding of the routine.

There is a distinction between teaching the meanings and principles of the operation and teaching the routines and algorithms. Foremost in the decision-making scheme is a determination of the needs of the students. Some relevant questions to consider are:

1. Have the students had an opportunity to develop meanings about the operation (addition, subtraction, multiplication, and division)?
2. To what extent does students' performance represent their "meanings" of the operation?
3. To what extent does students' performance show skill and capability with the operation?
4. To what extent does students' performance indicate differences between what they were taught and their actual work?
5. What is a good starting point for the students?

Another area to explore is the students' qualitative understanding of an operation. This exploration might begin with a discussion where students reveal sufficient information to enable you to identify their background experience and current understanding of the operations. Such a discussion may begin with the teacher asking questions similar to the following: "You have had addition in school. What can you tell me about what you have learned and how you learned it?" or "Can you tell me a time when you might subtract?" The focus of these and similar questions is to determine if the students can place the operation into an appropriate contextual setting that reflects a basic understanding of the operation.

The discussion should enable the teacher to determine the extent of the students' knowledge of the operation. If the student provides statements similar to "When you add, you put numbers together" or "When you add, you put numbers together to make a larger number" or "When you add, you put numbers together into a larger number that stands for all the smaller numbers," then you might conclude they have some understanding of addition. The latter would be a preferred answer, for it shows the students recognize that the sum of the parts is equal to and does not exceed the whole. Similar responses would provide information about the other operations.

Skill and capability with the operations should be evident by the speed, manner, and accuracy with which the students perform. Of these three factors, accuracy is probably of least concern when the students complete items of three, four, or more digits. For example, in 496×348, the opportunities for error are so numerous that students who are reasonably skillful with multiplication could produce an incorrect response. By contrast, computing 49×8 or 96×4 and other smaller combinations might be more indicative of skill. An orderly manner is important because it shows the students have control of the sequencing, spatiality, and interrelationships among place value. Finally, speed is important because it reflects the extent to which the students have internalized the operation and its processes.

The degree to which students show differences between what they were probably taught and their performance is algorithmic in character. When the students habitually demonstrate incorrect ways of calculating, the teacher can be reasonably assured that the methods were not directly taught to students. However, they might have developed because the students' work was not carefully monitored and every once in a while their method produced a correct answer. For example, students may solve $6\overline{)426}$ by saying, "Six into six is one." and write down the 1 as $\overset{1}{6\overline{)426}}$ and then say, "Six into forty-two is 7." and write in the 7 to show $\overset{71}{6\overline{)426}}$. In this instance the answer is correct. What would happen if the item had been $6\overline{)367}$? For reasons similar to the above, the teacher cannot always rely on the correct answer as evidence that the students know and understand the process.

What is a good starting point? A good starting point can only be determined by reviewing the samples of students' performance (e.g., the test items, daily assignments, etc.) within an available scope and sequence. This should begin by comparing the sequence of items that are correct with the sequence that is incorrect. Within the sequences one should compare the characteristics of the items that are correct to characteristics of those that are incorrect. The primary concern is the extent to which the students are making errors in algorithmic or representational use. Errors that are computational (e.g., $3 + 4 = 6$) should be dealt with by calling the students' attention to the item, indicating that it is incorrect and asking for an alternative response. The alternative correct response should be practiced.

Probability Control

The extent to which errors are likely to occur can be minimized by controlling the format of items. For example, we might begin with a two-choice option, proceed to a three-choice option, and then to an open-ended option. An example of this might look like:

	Format		Circle your choice.			
Monday	$3 + 4 =$	8	7			
Tuesday	$3 + 4 =$	7	6	9		
Wednesday	$3 + 4 =$	8	12	7	9	
Thursday	$3 + 4 =$	6	8	9	None of these	
Friday	$3 + 4 =$					

Controlled Repetition

Controlled repetition can also be used to teach targeted skills. The materials for addition with single-digit combinations could be given using a selection of sixty-four number combinations that are organized into thirty activity sheets that contain thirty-two items each. Example 1 would include sixteen activity sheets that have four different items where each item is repeated eight times. Example 17 would include the next eight activity sheets on which each has eight items that are repeated four times each. The next four activity sheets each have sixteen items and each item is repeated twice as in example 25. The two final activity sheets each have thirty-two different items and each item is presented once, as in example 29. The teacher can use either of the final two sheets, example 29, as a pretest or posttest. This type of structured repetition can be used in both power (i.e., no time limit) and speed (i.e., specified amount of time) conditions. The items for each page are listed so the teacher can use extended repetitions of any four combinations (e.g., example 1) or a lesser number of repetitions for combinations of items (e.g., example 17).

Worksheet 1

Name: _____
Teacher: _____
School: _____
Room Number: _____

7 +2	6 +2	4 +2

4 +2	7 +2	6 +2	5 +2

6 +2	5 +2	7 +2	6 +2	7 +2
5 +2	4 +2	5 +2	7 +2	4 +2
6 +2	5 +2	4 +2	5 +2	6 +2
4 +2	7 +2	4 +2	6 +2	7 +2
5 +2	4 +2	5 +2	7 +2	6 +2

Worksheet 17

Name: _____
Teacher: _____
School: _____
Room Number: _____

6 +2	8 +2	11 +2

5 +2	10 +2	7 +2	10 +2

4 +2	8 +2	6 +2	5 +2	11 +2
9 +2	4 +2	10 +2	8 +2	9 +2
8 +2	7 +2	5 +2	11 +2	7 +2
4 +2	6 +2	4 +2	9 +2	5 +2
11 +2	7 +2	9 +2	6 +2	10 +2

Worksheet 25

Name: _____
Teacher: _____
School: _____
Room Number: _____

12 +3	6 +3	8 +2

9 +2	4 +2	10 +2	11 +2

11 +3	5 +2	6 +2	8 +3	7 +2
8 +2	9 +3	5 +3	12 +3	10 +3
7 +3	10 +2	11 +3	8 +3	5 +2
4 +2	9 +2	6 +2	7 +3	9 +3
5 +3	7 +2	6 +3	11 +2	10 +3

Worksheet 29

Name: _____
Teacher: _____
School: _____
Room Number: _____

6 +4	12 +4	8 +2

7 +5	11 +2	7 +4	12 +3

10 +4	11 +4	6 +2	9 +5	13 +5
7 +3	10 +2	5 +3	8 +5	8 +3
10 +5	5 +2	8 +4	13 +4	12 +5
4 +2	6 +3	7 +2	10 +3	9 +2
11 +5	9 +3	14 +5	9 +4	11 +3

Active versus Passive Activities

In a relatively passive responding activity, students are provided with items and requested to provide responses. This is a learning activity with little or no interaction between the students and the items or between/among students. A more active format is for the teacher and students to discuss items that resemble 3 + 2 and 6 + 3. The students are then asked to "Make as many items as you can that have the same characteristics as those shown." Scoring can focus on fluency (i.e., number produced), accuracy (i.e., number correct), and originality (i.e., number that are different from one another). This type of activity can be done with any of the items listed in the computational sequences for the arithmetic operations in the appendix.

Error Detection Activities

To assist students in developing self-regulatory skills, activities in error detection and correction can be used as an integral facet of learning mathematics. For example the teacher could present students with a combination of items (e.g., 5 + 3 = 8, 9 + 6 = 14, 8 + 4 = 12, and 7 + 2 = 8) and ask them to determine which items are correct and which are incorrect. The students would be asked to first correct the incorrect items and then provide an explanation of the error they detected. This activity is easily extended to adding two- and three-digit numbers as well as any of the arithmetic operations or more advanced mathematical concepts.

Teaching Addition

Addition involves the principle that the sum of two or more numbers can be represented by a single larger number (e.g., 3 + 5 + 8 = 16) such that the total represents the sum of the parts. In a typical paper-pencil type activity, students often deal with addition items by writing a response without regard to the interrelationships among the whole and the parts. But, in real-life applications and activities the relationship between the parts and their sum is often emphasized and hard to overlook. One way to assist students in making the connection between real-life applications and paper-pencil activities is to incorporate both the "knowing" and "doing" of addition into learning activities and stress that there are many things to both "know about" and "do" addition.

It is important that addition be viewed as an operation that joins sets with equal or different amounts into a single set. Students should also know that addition is a mental activity in which numbers are added or combined. Sets or groups of objects or things are combined (e.g., show a pile of 3 apples and 5 oranges and ask, "How many pieces of fruit are there?"), where there is an intermediary step in which the representations of the objects are transposed into symbols (e.g., 3 and 5) and then recorded into a specific format to represent addition (i.e., 3 + 5 = 8).

To identify students' specific understanding of addition, an automatization assessment of single-digit combinations of numbers can be administered to separate what concepts are "known" from those that are "unknown." You might reexamine the table on pages 1 and 2 to review student performance on automatization items. Once the limits of students' knowledge are identified they should be given a set of problems that represent their specific "known" and asked to complete them as rapidly as possible to determine their level of automatization. The students should then be presented with two or three "unknowns" and asked to "figure them out" to the best of their ability. If the students' solutions do not reflect a sound mathematical solution process, a small set of items should be used to teach the targeted knowledge area. We suggest no more than four items from one specific knowledge or skill area at a time. Instruction should stress the development of a procedure or strategy that the students can generalize to "figure out" other unknowns. If the students fail to incorporate the procedure, then similar items from the same skill or knowledge area should be taught, always with the intent that the students will learn the procedure rather than the "facts."

Instruction of addition begins with single-digit numbers with sums of 9 or less. The real-life setting of the classroom should be used to initiate instructional activities by asking students to gather specified numbers of specific objects. One student might be asked to bring 3 red crayons and another student 5 blue crayons to the front table. Each student is likely to count to determine the cardinal property of a set and bring the specified items to the designated spot. The number of items brought by each student can be written on the board or a piece of paper and the addition can be conducted on the paper and then verified by the collection of crayons on the table. The teacher can then recap the activity and highlight the outcome by saying, "Jason brought three red crayons. Helen brought five blue crayons. Altogether, we have eight crayons. Who can tell us the number sentence without talking about the crayons?" This would lead into, "three plus five makes eight." At this point, the teacher might introduce one or two other combinations, rehearse them with the students, and then ask, "Can anyone think of another combination?" and use combinations generated by the students for other activities. Various combinations of games and competitions using a variety of representations should be provided to encourage students to develop speed and automaticity.

One common form of addition is a counting strategy that involves counting from the larger set through the smaller set. For example, when given 6 + 3, the students would say "six, seven, eight, nine." This was referred to previously as a form of "counting on." As students begin to remember certain combinations, they will use their memory to retrieve the appropriate answer. At other times, students may break an item down and add the components. For example, when given 5 + 6, students might say, "Five plus five is ten and one is eleven." It is important to observe the strategy or strategies the students use and to determine if the strategies are used correctly and effectively.

The transition from one- to two-digit number combinations should be accompanied by instruction that incorporates place value representations. This transition assumes an understanding that counting beyond 9 requires regrouping with objects or renaming with symbols, and can be presented in a series of formats that progress from sets of objects to expanded notation and finally to standard form similar to the following examples of 35 + 12 = 47 and 44 + 12 = 56.

	# = 10s and * = 1s	
Sets of Objects	### ***** + # ** #### *******	#### **** + # ** ##### ******
Expanded Notation	30 + 5 + 10 + 2 40 + 7	40 + 4 + 10 + 2 50 + 6
Standard Form	35 + 12 47	44 + 12 56

When renaming is required, the items can be presented in both expanded notation and standard form to highlight why and how renaming in the 1s column takes place. An example of this is provided below with the sums 36 + 18 = 54 and 47 + 15 = 62. Students can also represent these combinations with manipulatives and verbal explanations of both why and how they obtained a solution. Other combinations can be included, and each step in the combination can be controlled.

Expanded Notation		
	$30 + 6$	$40 + 7$
	$+\ 10 + 8$	$+\ 10 + 5$
	$40 + 14$	$50 + 12$
Standard Form		
	1	1
	36	47
	$+\ 18$	$+\ 15$
	54	62

Renaming in the 10s column requires knowledge of 100s, which should be developed prior to or along with the activity. For example, in $32 + 85 = 117$ and $43 + 84 = 127$ renaming takes place in the 10s column. And in $36 + 88 = 124$ and $47 + 84 = 131$ renaming takes place in both the 1s and 10s columns.

Renaming in the 10s column	Expanded Notation		
		$30 + 2$	$40 + 3$
		$+\ 80 + 5$	$+\ 80 + 4$
		$110 + 7$	$120 + 7$
	Standard Form		
		32	43
		$+\ 85$	$+\ 84$
		117	127
Renaming in the 1s and 10s column	Expanded Notation		
		$30 + 6$	$40 + 7$
		$+\ 80 + 8$	$+\ 80 + 4$
		$110 + 14$	$120 + 11$
	Standard Form		
		1	1
		36	47
		$+\ 88$	$+\ 84$
		124	131

Proceeding beyond renaming in the 1s and 10s columns involves a key decision related to the area of complexity in which to move. The complexity of the problems can be addressed by either extending the place value of the numbers used to the 100s (e.g., $324 + 312 = 636$) or to increase the number of rows and include more than two quantities (e.g., $23 + 41 + 15$). One element to note is that by increasing the number of rows or quantities it is possible to demonstrate both the associative and commutative properties of addition, specifically or on an intuitive level. The commutative property can be demonstrated by changing the number sequence so students can recognize that the order of the numbers being added can be changed without changing the result or answer (e.g., $23 + 41 + 15 = 79$, $41 + 15 + 23 = 79$, $15 + 41 + 23 = 79$, etc.).

Three-digit addition without renaming:	
	324
	$+\ 312$
	636
Adding three two-digit numbers	23
	41
	$+\ 15$
	79

A more important decision, particularly for students who have had difficulty with the traditional algorithm, is to consider teaching students an alternate algorithm to solving the problem. One alternative is to conduct the calculations from left to right. The background knowledge needed to introduce the left-to-right algorithm is set with instructional activities in place value and expanded notation conducted before arithmetic is introduced. The left-to-right algorithm can be presented using manipulative representations as a starting point, followed by expanded notation, and finally standard form, as in 324 + 312 = 636 demonstrated below.

Use of Manipulatives	Expanded Notation	Standard Form
^^^ ## ****	300 + 20 + 4	324
+ ^^^ # **	+ 300 + 10 + 2	+ 312
^^^^^^ ### ******	600	6
	300 + 20 + 4	324
	+ 300 + 10 + 2	+ 312
	600 + 30	63
	300 + 20 + 4	324
	+ 300 + 10 + 2	+ 312
	600 + 30 + 6	636

The inclusion of combinations beyond three-digit by three-digit numbers with renaming in the 100s, 10s, and 1s places have limited real-life value. In addition they are tedious, increase the opportunity for error, and have little or no value arithmetically if students effectively understand place value. When students are asked to work with items beyond the three-digit by three-digit number combinations, they should be taught to estimate the expected answer and then use a hand-held calculator to find an exact answer. Further, we suggest that the use of combinations beyond three digits be limited to real-life applications and problem-solving activities such as money or attendance during a sports tournament.

Teaching Subtraction

Subtraction is a process involving part-whole relationships and missing parts. The overriding principle in subtraction is that the whole is known and that part of it is missing or will be missing very soon. With this type of relationship there are three basic questions that can be asked. The three questions and an example of each are presented below.

Three Basic Questions or Situations Involved in Subtraction.

	Question	Example
1)	What remains of a quantity after part of it has been removed?	The teacher can place a set of objects on a table and ask a student to record the number of objects in the set. A second student can be asked to remove a number of objects from the set, and the first student can then record the number of objects removed. The students can then determine how many objects remain in the set. This process can be repeated and verified using the actual objects and/or the number of objects in the sets.

2)	What must be added to a quantity to make it as large as another quantity?	The teacher places one complete set and one incomplete set of objects on a table in front of the students. The teacher asks the students to determine the number of objects needed to complete the second set or incomplete set of objects. The teacher can also ask students to create their own example that is similar, where the second set of objects contains fewer objects than the first set.
3)	How much greater is one number than another?	The teacher places two sets of objects on a table and asks the students to count the number of objects in both sets. The students can then discuss which set is larger and use their counts of the number of objects in each set, to determine how much larger one set is than the other.

When appropriate, the teacher can create activities that reflect the three conditions or questions described above and ask the students to determine which condition each activity reflects. Each of the conditions can be addressed multiple times with a variety of materials and in various settings to help students identify the applications of subtraction and strengthen their skills in working with subtraction.

The overarching emphasis in subtraction is that it represents the difference between two numbers and that the relationship between the numbers can be expressed in a variety of forms. For example, the subtraction statement "eight minus two equals six" can be expressed with different elements missing and represented either horizontally (e.g., $8 - 2 = $ ___, $8 - $ ___ $= 6$, ___ $- 2 = 6$) or vertically.

$$\begin{array}{r} 8 \\ -2 \\ \hline 6 \end{array} \qquad \begin{array}{r} 8 \\ -? \\ \hline 6 \end{array} \qquad \begin{array}{r} ? \\ -2 \\ \hline 6 \end{array}$$

As was the case with addition, when initiating instruction in subtraction the teacher should first engage the students in a number of assessment activities to identify the specific knowledge they possess related to subtraction. What students "know" in subtraction can then be addressed to develop high levels of automaticity. The students can be taught various procedures or strategies to use when working with "unknowns" independently.

Students can also develop skills by working with multiple subtractions from the same minuend. That is, they should be given items such as: "Nadine has 13 apples. If she gives 4 apples to John, 3 to Helen, and 2 to Gus, how many apples will she have after each of her friends gets their apples?" This type of activity can also be used to demonstrate that there is often more than one way to solve a problem that involves more than two numbers or values (e.g., 29 –___ = ___ – ___ = 8; 29 –___ = ___ – ___ = ___).

The student can also engage in activities that emphasize estimation and proof where the teacher (a) places a set of items before them (e.g., 9 marbles), (b) has the students count the number of items, (c) takes some of the items away, (d) asks the students to estimate how many remain, and then (d) has the students count the number of items that were removed as proof. This activity should be conducted with sets that are a little larger in size than what students can count to rather easily and quickly.

A transition to the introduction of the more formal use of paper-pencil subtraction can take place if the teacher asks the students to record the number combinations for the respective activities. Initially the teacher can state the number combinations and their respective answers and then ask students to repeat his or her actions. As students become more familiar and comfortable with the process they can record the subtraction statements on their own. As the students begin to acquire a small number of "subtraction facts," the teacher can create numerous activities that would help enhance generalization. The teacher can then systematically introduce other combinations until the students know ten or twelve subtraction facts. Then the teacher might present students with an untaught combination and ask them to determine the answer. This can be expanded to a variety of representations through the Interactive Unit as previously illustrated.

Once the students demonstrate a firm understanding of subtraction and are able to complete single-digit combinations with ease, they should be given activities that will allow them to explore the relationship between addition and subtraction. For example students can be given addition and subtraction items (e.g., ___ + 3 = 9, 6 + ___ = 9, 6 + 3 = ___, 9 – ___ = 6, 9 – 3 = ___, ___ – 3 = 6) they can use to describe the relationships and use the relationships to help them interpret the "facts" table.

Students' understanding of the interrelationships among and between the arithmetic operations should be expanded as soon as single-digit subtraction is mastered. To do so, the teacher might present students with a set of items similar to the following:

```
   5        4        5        4
 + 2      + 3      - 2      - 3
   7        7        3        1
```

and ask why different number combinations yield the same answers. For example, "why is it that 5 + 2 and 5 – 2 have different answers?" And "why do 4 + 3 and 4 – 3 have different answers?" Ask students to both explain and demonstrate why this happens.

A major difficulty students have in subtracting is with renaming (Bryant, Bryant, & Hammill, 2000). For this reason, we recommend numerous manipulative activities that begin with a search for more objects than are available. This will facilitate the use of place value, as one object can represent ten of another type or color object. The teacher might extend this to the point of having to *borrow* items from another classroom, where the teacher has the available materials in sets of ten. The students should recognize that when they borrow in instances such as these, they will not use all of the items they originally borrowed.

A common error of young students when renaming is required is to avoid the process of renaming by taking the smaller digit from the larger digit regardless of its location (i.e., minuend and subtrahend). This type of error is shown in the following examples:

```
   90       426       856
 - 27     - 217     - 688
   77       211       232
```

Students who have had experience with place value and expanded notation should be asked to represent these items with manipulatives or other materials. Teachers will find that the students do not make the same error when they work with manipulatives. The task for the teacher is then to work with the students to align the steps between solving the problem with the manipulatives and expanded notation, emphasizing the importance of place value so that students understand the relationship between two formats of the same problem.

We recommend that instruction of two- and three-digit subtraction without renaming follow a sequence similar to that specified for addition, both of which are detailed in the appendix. A major difference when working with subtraction is that the teacher must continuously relate the problems to one of the three questions or situations stated at the beginning of this section on teaching subtraction. When shifting from two-digit items with renaming to items with three or more digits with renaming, particularly when there is renaming in both the 1s and 10s, it is important to make sure the students do not "borrow from the outside" for all renaming, as is demonstrated in the following example.

Borrowing from the Outside

Problem	Incorrect (borrow from the outside for all renaming)	Correct
5 3 2	3	1
− 2 5 4	4 1 1	4 2 1
2 7 8	5 3 2	5 3 2
	− 2 5 4	− 2 5 4
	1 8 8	2 7 8
5,2 3 5	2	1 1
− 2,3 5 7	3	4 1 2 1
2,8 7 8	4 1 1 1	5,2 3 5
	5,2 3 5	− 2,3 5 7
	− 2,3 5 7	2,8 7 8
	9 8 8	

Alternative Algorithms

This type of error can be quickly minimized with manipulatives and expanded notation. As students move from single-digit items to combinations of two or more digits, teachers face the continual decision of what algorithm to teach. Subtraction has many algorithms, and some appear more meaningful and easier than others. We suggest one, but recommend that others be explored.

Left-to-Right. The first algorithm we suggest is left-to-right. This is consistent with the use of left-to-right for addition and with the general reading process. The left-to-right algorithm accentuates the importance of place value and is consistent with estimation, which focuses on the digit farthest to the left. Examples without and with renaming follow.

Subtracting with and without Renaming

	Without Renaming		With Renaming	
Step 1	$50 + 2$ $\underline{-20 + 1}$ 30	$300 + 50 + 2$ $\underline{-100 + 20 + 1}$ 200	$50 + 2$ $\underline{-30 + 5}$ 20	$300 + 50 + 2$ $\underline{-100 + 30 + 5}$ 200
Step 2	$50 + 2$ $\underline{-20 + 1}$ $30 + 1$	$300 + 50 + 2$ $\underline{-100 + 20 + 1}$ $200 + 30$	$50 + 2$ $\underline{-30 + 5}$ $\cancel{20}$	$300 + 50 + 2$ $\underline{-100 + 30 + 5}$ $200 + \cancel{20}$
Step 3		$300 + 50 + 2$ $\underline{-100 + 20 + 1}$ $200 + 30 + 1$	$10 + 12$ $\underline{-\qquad 5}$ $10 + 7$	$200 + 10 + 12$ $\underline{-\qquad\qquad 5}$ $200 + 10 + 7$

Without Renaming. The without renaming algorithm bypasses renaming and allows the students to subtract using another process. Within a single place value when the digit in the subtrahend (i.e., the bottom line) is greater than the corresponding digit in the minuend (i.e., the top line) (e.g., the 4 is bigger than the 2, the 5 is bigger than the 3), rewrite the minuend (i.e., the top line) using the following rule.

423 $\underline{-145}$ 278	Original Problem
399 $\cancel{423}$ $\underline{-145}$ $254 \quad (399 - 145)$ $\underline{+\ \ 24} \quad (423 - 399)$ 278	Take the digit in the highest place value position in the minuend (i.e., 4) and rewrite it as one smaller (i.e., 4 goes to 3). Write the remaining digits in the minuend as 9s. Then subtract the subtrahend from the new minuend. Add back what was taken away (i.e., 23 + 1 [423 − 399 = 24]) and you have your answer.

This algorithm is particularly helpful when subtracting numbers that involve zero as is shown in the following example:

299 $\cancel{306}$ $\underline{-157}$ $142 \quad (299 - 157)$ $\underline{+\ \ 7} \quad (306 - 299)$ 149	$2{,}999$ $\cancel{3{,}006}$ $\underline{-1{,}578}$ $1{,}421 \quad (2{,}999 - 1{,}578)$ $\underline{+\qquad 7} \quad (3{,}006 - 2{,}999)$ $1{,}428$

    The questions concerning the use of alternative algorithms relate to (a) the extent to which the students use a portion or all of an alternative algorithm, (b) the extent to which the students are confused with the traditional algorithm, or (c) the extent to which the teacher wants the students to know different ways to do computations. This, of course, is a question that can only be answered by the district, school, or teacher.

Teaching Multiplication

Multiplication is a process of joining a collection of sets all having the same number of objects. Two principles that guide multiplication instruction are the many-to-one representation and the factor × factor = product relationship. The many-to-one principle stipulates that one unit is represented many times. That is, a unit of 4 may be represented 6 times in the form of $6 \times 4 =$ ___ or a unit of 142 may be represented 6 times in the form $6 \times 142 =$ ___. The factor × factor = product relationship expresses multiplication as the relationship between the factors (i.e., the numbers being multiplied together) and the product (i.e., answer). The relationship between the factors and the product can be seen in an example like $6 \times 4 = 24$. In terms of multiplication, the relationship can be written as either $6 \times 4 =$ ___ or $4 \times 6 =$ ___, and in division it can be written as $6 \overline{)24}$ or $4 \overline{)24}$. These expressions represent the commutative property of multiplication as well as the relationship between multiplication and division. The factors can be expanded to a variety of combinations such as $3 \times 2 \times 2 \times 2$, $2 \times 3 \times 2 \times 2$, $2 \times 2 \times 3 \times 2$, or $2 \times 2 \times 2 \times 3$ and expressed in alternative forms such as $(3 \times 2) \times (2 \times 2)$, $3 \times (2 \times 2) \times 2$, or $3 \times 2 \times (2 \times 2)$. Over the course of their instruction in multiplication, the students should be exposed to many of these and other forms of representation.

Multiplication can be presented as $6 \times 4 = 24$ and $4 \times 6 = 24$. Its interrelationship to division can be shown as $6 \times$ ___ $= 24$ and ___ $\times 4 = 24$. Another way is to express the relationship as $\underset{}{}\overset{6}{\overline{)24}}$ and $\underset{}{}\overset{4}{\overline{)24}}$.

Many students experience great difficulty in trying to learn multiplication. Major areas of students' difficulty involve "knowing the tables," and managing the sheer number of steps and rules that need to be followed when working with complex number combinations (e.g., 496×348). As with subtraction and division, careful attention must be paid to the individual steps, the sequence of steps, and the subsequent answer when multiplying.

Initial instruction in multiplication typically involves skip counting, which works well when working with small numbers. But as the numbers or quantities increase in value so does the difficulty of working with skip counting. To work with larger numbers effectively students need to learn other methods of multiplication in order to work with related calculations. When teaching multiplication beyond skip counting, a major instructional decision is whether the traditional algorithm that focuses on paper-pencil use will be the dominant if not the only method taught or if instruction will also include alternative methods of multiplying.

Instruction should begin with an assessment of students' ability to multiply correctly. This can be done by giving students a series of items that progress in difficulty based on the number of digits in each factor and the level of carrying that is required within the calculations, see the appendix for a sample series. If the students perform satisfactorily, in both speed and accuracy (i.e., at or above 80 percent correct), on the assessment, then the method they used to solve the individual problems should be examined. If the students only lack speed, then a number of speed drill activities can be developed to address this area. If the students do not perform satisfactorily in both speed and accuracy, then instruction should begin as though the students do not know multiplication.

Instruction in multiplication of single-digit numbers often focuses on the "tables" at the expense of highlighting the relationship among the combinations of numbers. The "tables" tend to dominate, and practicing the tables becomes more important than learning how to construct the tables, which can reflect a deeper understanding of multiplication than sheer memorization of the "facts." Introduction of the "tables" and "facts" should begin with numerous hands-on experiences using varying numbers of sets with the same number of objects. The teacher might first show four trees, each with three apples and ask the students to skip count to determine the number of apples on all three trees. As the students become skillful with skip counting, the teacher might say, "There is also another way we can count the apples. Let me show you. There are three apples on each tree and there are four trees. So we can say, "four times three equals twelve." This is faster than saying "three plus three plus three plus three equals twelve." A key concept in this activity is to emphasize that "times" is another way to "skip count" and that the rule for skip counting, (i.e., each set has the same number of items) is the general principle for multiplication.

The relationship between skip counting and "times" can be further developed using some directed activities that highlight the relationship between the size and number of elements in a sequence. Instruction can begin by asking students to write a skip-counting sequence for 2. The students might write, 2, 4, 6, 8 and indicate that the final value represents the number of "skips." Then ask students if they can rewrite the sequence using the "times" approach (i.e., 4×2). Students can then be asked to use some objects and demonstrate that the "skip-counting" and "times" approaches yield the same result. Then students can be asked to create a skip-counting sequence for 3, beginning with 3 and using a collection of objects. Students can then be asked to build a skip-counting sequence for 3 beginning with 2 (i.e., $3 \times 2 = 6$). Ultimately the focus of the activities is to develop the understanding that each subsequent increase in a skip (e.g., 3, 6, 9, etc.) increases the value by the amount of the unit.

Once the students understand skip counting and its relationship to multiplication, the teacher should introduce the identity element (or multiplicative identity property) and the multiplication property of zero, which involve multiplying by 1 and 0 respectively. The multiplicative identity element indicates that any number multiplied by 1 is the number. Thus, $7 \times 1 = 7$; $32 \times 1 = 32$; and $357 \times 1 = 357$. The multiplicative identity element can be demonstrated by using a number of containers (e.g., jars) and placing a certain number of the same type of object (e.g., marbles or toothpicks) into one container at a time. Ask the students to count the number of objects as you put them into the containers. Help the students to understand that if they have only 1 jar and the jar contains 5 marbles then they still have 5 marbles (i.e., $1 \times 5 = 5$). Thus "any number times one is that number" or "one times any number is that number." Similarly, if no objects are placed in the container, the students have nothing (i.e., $1 \times 0 = 0$). If 4 jars are displayed and there are no objects in any of the jars, there is nothing in any of the jars to multiply (i.e., $4 \times 0 = 0$). Therefore, we say, "Any number times zero is zero." It is important to keep in mind that in multiplication, as in addition and subtraction, zero serves only as a placeholder. The use of activities that involve "hands-on" and manipulative representations may be needed to help students grasp the difficult concepts involved in multiplication.

Alternative Representations

Representing the multiplication of single-digit combinations of numbers with manipulatives or pictures of objects is relatively quick and simple. This is frequently done by describing multiplication as a way to determine the total number of items in a collection of sets that have the same number of items. For example four sets with three in each set shows four times three or 4×3 as reflected in the following example.

xxx   xxx   xxx   xxx

Students can then compare the same combination of various items, as shown below, as a way to help them develop the generalization that "four times two is eight."

∧∧ ∧∧   ∧∧ ∧∧   ## ## ## ##   ** ** ** **

The teacher can then display different combinations of items and ask the students to verbalize and then write the combinations. A combination of illustrations similar to the ones shown below can be created by students as a way to visualize the multiplication facts. The teacher can emphasize the use of the pictographs by saying, "If you have this many in a set [points to ###] and you have this many sets [points to 2], draw pictures to show how many items you have all together." The students can then complete and/or expand the chart as a way to create a visual representation of the multiplication table.

Illustration of Some of the Multiplication Facts

		Number of Items in a Set				
		#	##	###	####	#####
	1	#				
Number	2			###		
of				###		
Sets	3		##			#####
			##			#####
			##			#####
	4				####	
					####	
					####	
					####	

Array Multiplication

Instruction in multiplication can also be done using arrays as a way to stress the interrelationships among the individual multiplication facts. The use of arrays also enables us to do multiplication using a counting algorithm, which can highlight the fact that multiplication is a form or repeated addition. As with other activities, multiplication using arrays can begin with manipulatives and then translated into symbolic form using numbers. An example, an array of five times six and its rotated counterpart, six times five, is shown below.

Array Multiplication Example

5×6	6×5
######	#####
######	#####
######	#####
######	#####
######	#####
	#####

When carrying out multiplication calculations the commutative property holds and the answer will be the same regardless of the order in which the numbers are multiplied. Provide the students with sets of objects and ask one group of students to organize the objects into six sets with five objects in each set. Ask another group of students to organize the objects into five sets with six objects in each set. Call attention to the fact that each group of students has the same total number of objects (i.e., thirty).

Use the array of five times six and ask the students to identify other ways that the array can be represented, as shown in the example below.

Array Multiplication Example

5×6	$(2 \times 6) + (3 \times 6)$	$(3 \times 6) + (2 \times 6)$	$(1 \times 6) + (4 \times 6)$	$(4 \times 6) + (1 \times 6)$
xxxxxx	xxxxxx	xxxxxx	xxxxxx	xxxxxx
xxxxxx	xxxxxx	xxxxxx		xxxxxx
xxxxxx		xxxxxx	xxxxxx	xxxxxx
xxxxxx	xxxxxx		xxxxxx	xxxxxx
xxxxxx	xxxxxx	xxxxxx	xxxxxx	
	xxxxxx	xxxxxx	xxxxxx	xxxxxx

Work with students to develop the idea that "five times six" can be written as "one times six plus four times six." Put the array back in its original five-times-six format and ask the students to show different ways of representing, "five times six." They may come up with a number of combinations that may include "2×6 plus 3×6," or even "2×6 plus 2×6 plus 1×6."

Teaching multiplication using arrays leads very nicely into the distributive property of multiplication over addition which has numerous implications for teaching the "tables." Given that the students know the role of "1" as the identity element (i.e., any number times 1 is the number) and understand that multiplication by zero results in zero, the distributive property provides great flexibility in working with combinations of numbers. For example students only need to memorize three tables, the 2s, 5s, and 10s. The distributed property can then be used to demonstrate that all of the other multiplication tables can be derived from knowing these three tables. The 8s table can be derived as the 10s table minus the 2s table (e.g., $8 \times 3 = (10 \times 3) - (2 \times 3)$) and the 7s table is the 5s table plus the 2s table (e.g., $7 \times 4 = (5 \times 4) + (2 \times 4)$). By knowing the 2s, 5s, and 10s tables and using the distributive property, the students can construct any combination of multiplication facts and if necessary all the tables.

Once students demonstrate an accurate understanding of the relationship between the various multiplication tables, they can engage in activities designed to help them habituate targeted tables. One such activity involves the factor $\times$ factor = product aspect of multiplication as in "six times three equals eighteen" (i.e., $6 \times 3 = \underline{\quad}$, $\underline{\quad} \times 3 = 18$, and $6 \times \underline{\quad} = 18$). The students can also identify the missing factor for specified combinations or complete an array when given combinations as in the following example.

Missing Factors in Array Multiplication

$\times$	2	4	6	8
3				
5				
7				

It is important that students see the interrelationships among a number of different factors and a product. They should do activities such as $3 \times 2 \times 2$; $4 \times 3 \times 2$; $3 \times 2 \times 2 \times 3$ as well as $3 \times 2 \times ? = 12$; $5 \times ? \times 2 = 30$ to expand or clarify their understanding of the interrelationships among numbers.

Combinations of Two or More Digits

The shift from multiplying single-digit combinations to combinations involving two or more digits must involve place value. For this, we can return to the use of arrays and create manipulative representations of selected combinations similar to "three times twenty-three" and "two times two hundred fourteen," as in the example below. Because this can become cumbersome, it should be done only with multiplicands having place value to the thousands and single-digit multipliers (e.g., the maximum would be thousands multiplied by 9). After the students are able to recognize the combinations and can state and/or create them when given oral instructions, the teacher can move on to expanded notation and then standard form, as in the following example.

	3×23	2×214
Manipulative Representation	## ***	^^ # ****
	## ***	^^ # ****
	## ***	
Expanded Notation	$20 + 3$	$200 + 10 + 4$
	$20 + 3$	$200 + 10 + 4$
	$20 + 3$	
Standard Form	23	214
	$\times\ \underline{3}$	$\times\ \underline{2}$
	69	428

Both the manipulative and expanded notation illustrations show the students how to count through multiplication. Once the students have demonstrated mastery and speed with these types of items, it is then appropriate to introduce renaming. Renaming can be demonstrated with manipulatives and expanded notation as shown in the example below. This can be done by extending the above examples into items like the following that involve regrouping.

Problem Format	Renaming	4×23	3×214
Manipulative Representation	Without	## ***	^^ # ****
		## ***	^^ # ****
		## ***	^^ # ****
		## ***	^^^^^ ### ***********
		######## ***********	
	With	#	#
		## **	^^ # **
		##	^^ #
		##	^^ #
		##	^^^^^ #### **
		######### **	
Expanded Notation	Without	20 + 3	200 + 10 + 4
		20 + 3	200 + 10 + 4
		20 + 3	200 + 10 + 4
		20 + 3	600 + 30 + 12
		60 + 12	
	With	10	10
		20 + 2	200 + 10 + 2
		20	200 + 10
		20	200 + 10
		20	600 + 40 + 2
		90 + 2	

At this point the students should have the capability to make the transition to written and spoken items in standard form that do not involve renaming similar to the examples below.

$$\begin{array}{r} 23 \\ \times\ 3 \\ \hline 69 \end{array} \qquad \begin{array}{r} 214 \\ \times\ 2 \\ \hline 428 \end{array}$$

Items having these and other characteristics should be presented in both spoken and written forms as a way to further strengthen students' multiplication skills. The students should be asked to solve the items, make representations of them, and explain the steps involved in solving the items. At the very least, the students should be able to multiply two-digit by single-digit items without paper and pencil. They should also be able to multiply three- and four-digit items by single-digit items at about the same rate per step as it takes to multiply two single-digit items. For example, students should be able to do 2×214 with the same speed that they can do 2×2, 2×1, 2×4, and $4 + 2 + 8$, for each has the same number of steps.

Once multiplication of multidigit by single-digit items without renaming is mastered, it is important to emphasize the role of place value in order to multiply multi- and single-digit numbers that involve renaming. It is important that the students work with items such as 12×348 and realize that they can split the values up (e.g., $(10 \times 348) + (2 \times 348)$) to simplify the multiplication process. It is the $10 + 2$ that creates the two-digit by three-digit spatiality where the students have to "move over."

A	B
348	348
$\times 12$	$\times 12$
696	3,480
$+ 3,480$	$+ \ \ \ 696$
4,176	4,176

It is our sense that students should learn the format presented in column A for multiplication before the format in column B, and they should learn format B as another way of doing format A. Format A is a fine way of doing multiplication and should be encouraged and maintained. It is important that the students recognize the two formats as "one and the same," and that the dropping of the zero is a "timesaver" and not a different routine.

Multiplication is the one operation that increases the potential for error most significantly as the number of steps in the routine increase. Errors are largely computational, and for the most part, the errors made by the different students will have no substantial pattern. It is important therefore, that the teacher examines each item completed by students for algorithmic versus computational errors.

$$
\begin{array}{rl}
12 \times 235 = 2400 & (12 \times 200) \\
360 & (12 \times 30) \\
+ \ \ \ 60 & (12 \times 5) \\
\hline
2,820 &
\end{array}
$$

We suggest students use hand-held calculators once they have mastered the algorithm because by increasing the size of the items the opportunities for errors also increases and the error pattern often becomes meaningless. To guard against keying in incorrect digit combinations estimation should also be emphasized whenever calculators are used. It would be much better to give a two-item worksheet and ask the students to complete the items using different methods than to give students ten to fifteen items and ask them to solve the different items using only one method. Another option is to give half the students 496×348 and another half 348×496 and ask each group to solve their respective item. The two groups could then compare their answers and partial products and discuss the similarities and differences between their solutions and explain why they exist.

Estimation

Estimation is an important capability for multiplication. Asking for help or passing on an item because they have a specific unanswered question should be viewed as an advanced level of executive behavior such as monitoring one's performance. It is better for the students to ask for help or choose not to complete an item than to try to solve it in a meaningless way. Worksheets and similar tasks should include an option for the students to ask for help or to specify a question related to completing an item. In fact, as much as we criticize it, so is using one's fingers, for it indicates that the students recognize that they do not know, but that they have devised an alternative means of finding out.

Estimating an item such as 496×348 assumes some degree of ability in working with place value with large numbers and with zero as a placeholder. The development of facility with estimation should begin early *and* be an integral component to all activities in both computation and problem solving. Assuming that students understand estimation and that they have used it with addition and subtraction, estimation for multiplication can follow the same principles. First, estimation is done from left-to-right. In this instance the students must first identify the 4 in 496 as 400 and the 3 in 348 as 300. The students must understand that the multiplication process is going to result in a "big" number that has as many digits as the total number of zeros in 300 and 400 combined plus the 3×4.

Estimation can also be emphasized in worksheet activities as shown below. Such activities can be developed for each of the arithmetic operations to help emphasize that estimation is an important and valuable skill in reviewing calculations. Overall, estimation should be taught as a separate process according to the guidelines of the district.

Name:_____   Date:_____

Instructions: Complete all the items on the page. Write your estimated answer in the space provided before you complete the item. Match your estimated answer to your actual answer.

Item	Estimated Answer	Actual Answer
13 × 4	50	52
326 × 5	1,500	1,630
428 × 74	28,000	31,672

Algorithmic Variations

In addition to the use of alternative representations, multiplication also offers opportunities for the use of algorithmic modifications. Calculators and computers input numbers from left-to-right, and we should be aware that multiplication can be done not only from left-to-right, but from any starting position. Examine the following item in both expanded notation and in the use of alternative starting points where A = 100s, B = 10s, and C = 1s.

Algorithmic Variations in Multiplication

Original Item	Expanded Notation	Alternative Starting Points			
		A to B to C	B to A to C	C to B to A	B to C to A
343	300 + 40 + 3	343	343	343	343
× 2		× 2	× 2	× 2	× 2
686	× _____ 2	600	80	6	80
	600 + 80 + 6	80	600	80	6
		+ 6	+ 6	+ 600	+ 600
		686	686	686	686

Teaching Division

An assessment of students' needs in division is also taken first from a test of combinations of single-digit numbers. If the students have performed satisfactorily (i.e., at or above 80 percent correct), then their solutions to the items on the proficiency tests should be examined to ensure they are using appropriate strategies. If the students only lack speed, then a number of speed drill activities can be developed to address this area. If the students do not perform satisfactorily in both speed and accuracy, then instruction should begin as though the students do not know division.

Division is a process in which students seek to determine either measurement or partitioning. Measurement involves the question, "how many groups?" while partitioning asks, "how many in each group?" (Reisman, 1977). An example of measurement division is to present students with a problem similar to the following: "There are 12 oranges. Three oranges will be given to each person. How many people will get oranges?" An example of partitive division is to ask students to solve a problem similar to the following: "There are 12 oranges. The oranges will be divided evenly among 4 people. How many oranges will each person get?"

Instruction in division should include numerous meaningful activities to assist the students in learning how to differentiate between the measurement and partitioning applications of division. This is an important distinction for students to make in order to attain proficiency in division.

The teacher might begin with a measurement activity such as an ocean scene and a number of different sea animals (e.g., whales, walruses, swordfish, and sharks). A "set" of oceans can be placed before the students with a certain number of animals (e.g., 2 ocean scenes and 4 sharks). The students can be asked to place 2 sharks in each ocean or to place the same number of sharks in each ocean. For the first task, one would expect the students to put 2 sharks in one ocean and then place 2 sharks in the other ocean. For the second task, the students might put one shark in each ocean until all the sharks are evenly distributed between the two oceans. Observe the strategy that students use and ask them to describe or explain the strategy in order to determine the extent to which it is reliable and meaningful.

The instructional setting can shift to partitioning when the teacher provides the students with a set of objects (e.g., 9 sea animals) and asks the students to determine how many oceans are needed to put 3 animals in each ocean. One possible strategy is for the students to take one ocean and place 3 animals in it, and then repeat the activity until the 9 sea animals are distributed.

At this point it would be appropriate to introduce the formal concept of division as specifying the number of sets contained in a sum or product, or when given the number of sets, its the size of each set. The word "set" should be used in order to avoid the traditional "can't go into" that is commonly used when dividing with two-digit dividends. Ordinarily, division is the only arithmetic operation that is traditionally taught using a left-to-right algorithm. However, we have already indicated that all the operations can be done left-to-right, and it is possible, therefore, that this will not be novel to the students.

As the students prepare and respond to different representations of division, their attention should be directed to spoken and written formats. In discussing the various introductory activities, the teacher can use the nomenclature of division as a way to familiarize students with language related to division. Accordingly, when introducing skills that build up to division, terms such as "sets with this many," "this many sets," and so forth should be used to facilitate instruction with formal division notation. We will see the value of this momentarily.

After the introduction of the nomenclature, the teacher should begin to make the transition from spoken and manipulative representations to various written forms. The first and most traditional of written forms is $\overline{)}$. Transition to symbol notation can be done by making connections to addition, subtraction, or multiplication symbols that are familiar to the students. The traditional symbol for division (i.e., $\overline{)}$) and the vocabulary terms of the quantities involved can be introduced (i.e., divisor, dividend, and quotient). The teacher can then demonstrate how to read or interpret the combination of numbers that accompany the symbol (e.g., $3\overline{)6}$). For example the teacher might say, "How many sets can I make with this many in each set [pointing to divisor, i.e., 3] if I have this number of items [pointing to dividend, i.e., 6]?" It is also important to show students how to write or record their answer to a division problem presented in the traditional format as a way to facilitate working with larger numbers in the future. The process should be repeated with various combinations of single-digit numbers that do not involve renaming, until the students can solve the problems without hesitating or resorting to counting.

Present students with a collection of division problems and ask them to use the available manipulatives to make representations of the items. Select a few of the students' representations and ask them to write down what they have created using the traditional format for division. For example on being shown $3\overline{)12}$, students would arrange items as follows:

$3\overline{)12}$ XXX   XXX   XXX   XXX

To move on to dividing single-digit numbers into two-digit numbers without remainders, it is necessary to return to place value. Begin the sequence by using any two sets of items (e.g., toothpicks and paper clips) and placing them before the students. Ask the students to group the objects in each pile into sets of a given size (e.g., "Make as many sets as you can with two paper clips in each set and do the same with the toothpicks"). And then write the problem as in the following example.

Given:	###### ********	* = 1s; # = 10s
Make:	## ## ## ** ** ** **	
Traditional Division Format:	$2\overline{)68}$	

If the students demonstrate each step of the activity correctly, provide them with similar problems that involve different combinations of numbers. If the students carry out any of the steps incorrectly, the teacher should guide the students by modeling each of the steps in the activity. The procedure can then be reversed where students are given symbolic representations of division and asked to create manipulative representations of the items as in the example below.

Traditional Division Format $\quad\quad\quad\quad\quad\quad$ $3\overline{)39}$
Manipulative Representation $\quad\quad\quad\quad\quad$ ### *********
$\quad\quad\quad\quad\quad\quad\quad\quad\quad\quad\quad\quad\quad\quad$ * = 1s; # = 10s

When representing division problems using manipulatives the students should be provided with 100s as ten 10s, 10s as ten 1s, and ones as 1s. The above example should be followed with another similar to $4\overline{)12}$ where students have to determine how to divide the total (i.e., 12) into sets with 4 in each set. The students should recognize that the 10s must be unwrapped and regrouped into ten 1s, which will then make a set of twelve 1s. The key factor is to regroup the 10s into 1s. This will help later when working with partial dividends. Provide students with various combinations of numbers such as $3\overline{)24}$, $4\overline{)16}$, and $5\overline{)25}$, but do not include items with remainders. Complete this activity with items such as $3\overline{)24}$ and $3\overline{)36}$ where combinations of regrouping and no regrouping are used. Be certain the students know when they need to regroup and when they do not.

To highlight the relationship between division and multiplication, systematically present a sequence of items using one multiplication table (e.g., $2\overline{)4}$, $2\overline{)6}$, $2\overline{)8}$, $2\overline{)10}$). Use the sequence of the number combinations to call attention to the relationship between division and multiplication. Indicate that when you ask, "How many twos are in four?" you are also asking, "What is two times two?" Use the relationship between multiplication and division to present students with combinations of items that use another form of division as in the example below.

$2 \times \underline{\quad} = 4$	$4 \div 2 = \underline{\quad}$
$\underline{\quad} \times 3 = 6$	$\underline{\quad} \div 3 = 2$
$2 \times 4 = \underline{\quad}$	$8 \div \underline{\quad} = 4$
$\underline{\quad} \times 5 = 10$	$10 \underline{\quad} 5 = 2$

Call attention to the new way of writing division (i.e., ÷) and show the students that they now have two ways to write division (i.e., $2\overline{)4}$ and 4 ÷ 2). It is also important to discuss with students how to say or describe the two formats of division. For example they would usually say, "How many twos are in four?" for the first form and "Four divided by two" for the second form. Show examples of the relationship between multiplication and division with matrices such as the one shown below.

× ÷	1	2	3	4	5
1	1	2	3	4	5
2	2	4	6	8	10
3	3	6	9	12	15

Show how multiplication of 2 and 3 (e.g., 2 × 3) will intersect at 6 and that if they had 2 and 6, 3 would be the missing factor, so that 6 divided by 2 would be 3.

At this point the students should be relatively skilled with single-digit division. Discuss with students the value of recalling some of the combinations quickly. A variety of approaches (e.g., worksheet sequences, flash cards, games, etc.) can be used to facilitate memorizing or recalling the division "facts" quickly.

Remainders

Present the students with an item such as $2\overline{)5}$ and ask them to create a representation of the problem using manipulatives or by drawing a representation of the problem. The students' representation should resemble something like the image below.

＊＊   ＊＊   ＊

Then ask the students to circle the sets that can be created if each set contains two items. Call attention to the single unit and ask students for suggestions as to what can be done with the extra item. As part of the discussion the teacher can highlight the concept of a remainder because it does not make a full set of two. To extend the presence of a remainder from working with manipulatives to paper and pencil forms of division it is important to emphasize that the remainder is written in a specific way (e.g., $3\overline{)11}^{3R2}$). Students can then practice the notation by solving similar items.

Division with single-digit and three-digit numbers or larger can then be explored using manipulatives to help students generalize their knowledge of division. The teacher can ask the students to solve $3\overline{)396}$ (step 1 in the problem shown below) by creating a manipulative representation for the problem (step 2). Ask the student to circle as many sets with this many (pointing to divisor, ***) in each set for each item (i.e., \$, #, and 1). Explain that the number that represents the specified number of sets in each place value location is to show there is one set of 3 for the 100s, three sets of 3 for the 10s, and two sets of 3 for the 1s (step 3). After practicing similar items, students can be introduced to the traditional symbolic form (step 4). In discussing the process used to solve the problem, indicate that both the symbolic and manipulative forms of division used to represent the problem are equivalent and they are just different ways of showing division. With either format the question asked is, "How many sets can I make with this many [3] in each set [sets of 100s, sets of 10s, sets of 1s]." This same solution process can also be used when working with division statements that involve remainders in the 1s column (e.g., $4\overline{)489}$).

Step	
1	$3\overline{)396}$
2	$111\overline{)\$\$\$\#\#\#\#\#\#\#\#\#111111}$
3	$\qquad$ 1 $\qquad$ 3 $\qquad$ 2
	$111\overline{)\$\$\$\#\#\#\#\#\#\#\#\#111111}$
4	$\dfrac{132}{3\overline{)396}}$

Key: \$ = 100's; # = 10's; and 1 = 1's

Moving Over

Traditional instructional approaches in division often use phrases such as "___ does not go into ___, so we move over." An example would be $3\overline{)123}$ where the teacher might say, "Three into one does not go, so we move over." But to make such a statement is not fully accurate because the 1 in 123 represents 100, the 2 represents 20, and the 3 represents 3. Certainly 3 goes into 100, 20, and 3. A more accurate statement would be, "How many sets with this many in each set [3] can you make from this many [100]?" This can be represented using manipulatives as shown in the example below (step 2). The teacher can then ask the students to show how many sets of three 100s can be made if they only have one 100. Since there is only one 100, no sets with three in each set can be made. The teacher can then encourage students to regroup the set of 100, into ten 10s (step 3). At this point the problem shows twelve 10s and students are asked to determine how many sets of three can they make with the twelve 10s. The students can count four sets of three 10s and write the number (step 4). Students can then determine the number of sets of three that can be made in the 1s, which should be 1 (step 5). Continue to work with students to make the transition from the pictorial representation to the traditional symbolic form (step 6).

Step	
1	$3\overline{)123}$
2	$111\overline{)\$\#\#111}$
3	$111\overline{)\#\#\#\#\#\#\#\#\#\#\#\#111}$
4	$\overset{4}{111\overline{)\#\#\#\#\#\#\#\#\#\#\#\#111}}$
5	$\overset{4\quad\quad1}{111\overline{)\#\#\#\#\#\#\#\#\#\#\#\#\,11}}$
6	$3\overline{)123}^{\,41}$

Key: $ = 100's; # = 10's; and 1 = 1's

If the students have difficulty making the transition to the symbolic form, model the verbalization of the sequence of steps by saying, "This [pointing to symbolic representation] is another way of writing this [pointing to pictorial representation]. We say the same thing, but the only difference is that we do it with number symbols. First, we say, 'How many sets with this many 100s [pointing to the 3] in each set can we make here [pointing to 1 in 100]?' We cannot make any sets with three 100s in a set, so we have to rename the one 100 as ten 10s. The only difference is that we don't need to write the renaming, we can just think it (in other words, we have twelve 10s). So now we can ask, 'How many sets with three in each set can we make here [pointing to the 12]?' Four sets of three can be created from 12, so we write 4 above the 10s place." Point to the three in the 1s position and ask, "How many sets with three in each set can we make here? One set of three can be created from 3 and so we write 1 above the 1s place."

Students should do a number of similar items until they can demonstrate the solution using manipulatives or pictorial representations and the traditional symbolic notation. They should also be able to readily explain the meaning and routine of the solution process.

Regrouping Partial Dividends

Most students do not realize that remainders exist as partial dividends. In addition, they do not understand the relationships that exist among the various components of the traditional long division format. A demonstration is provided in the following problem, where students are asked to describe the item and the solution process used to solve it. When the students are presented with the problem (step 1) they should say something similar to "This shows 3 into 45" (step 1). "We need to find out how many sets of 3 are in 45. First, we have to find out how many sets of 3 we can make with the 10s. We have one set of 3 in 40 and we have one set of 10 left over" (step 2).

Step	
1	$111\overline{)\#\#\#\#11111}$
2	$\phantom{111\overline{)}}1$ $111\overline{)\#\#\#\#11111}$
3	$\phantom{111\overline{)}}1$ $111\overline{)\#\#\#11111111111111}$
4	$\phantom{111\overline{)}}15$ $111\overline{)\#\#\#11111111111111}$
5	$\phantom{3\overline{)}}15$ $3\overline{)45}$
6	$\phantom{3\overline{)}}1$ $3\overline{)45}$
7	$\phantom{3\overline{)}}1$ $3\overline{)45}$ $\phantom{3\overline{)}}3$ (Keep this in mind as $10 \times 3 = 30$)
8	$\phantom{3\overline{)}}1$ $3\overline{)45}$ $\phantom{3\overline{)}}\underline{-3}$ (Keep this in mind as $10 \times 3 = 30$) $\phantom{3\overline{)}}1$
9	$\phantom{3\overline{)}}1$ $3\overline{)45}$ $\phantom{3\overline{)}}\underline{-3}$ (Keep this in mind as $10 \times 3 = 30$) $\phantom{3\overline{)}}15$ $(10 + 5 = 15)$
10	$\phantom{3\overline{)}}15$ $3\overline{)45}$ $\phantom{3\overline{)}}\underline{-3}$ $\phantom{3\overline{)}}15$ $\phantom{3\overline{)}}15$
11	$\phantom{3\overline{)}}15$ $3\overline{)45}$ $\phantom{3\overline{)}}\underline{-3}$ $\phantom{3\overline{)}}15$ $\phantom{3\overline{)}}\underline{-15}$ $\phantom{3\overline{)}}0$

Key: $ = 100's; # = 10's; and 1 = 1's

If the students do not know what to do with the leftover 10, assist by modeling the remainder of the item. Say, "We have a 10 here. We cannot make another set with the 10s because we only have one 10. But we can take the one 10 that is by itself and regroup it to make ten 1s" (step 3). "We can then see how many sets of 3 we can make out of the fifteen 1s. Five sets of 3 can be made from the fifteen 1s" (step 4). The problem can then be written in traditional symbolic form as $3\overline{)45}^{\,15}$ (step 5).

The solution process using the traditional symbolic notation can then be developed. Ask the students to complete the item and explain their steps as they go. The students should say something like, "Forty-five divided by 3 asks how many sets with 3 in each set are in 45. First, we have to find out how many sets of 3 we have in the 10s. We can make one set of 3 and we have one 10 left over" (step 6). At this point, the students may not know that subtraction is necessary to address the remaining 10. The teacher can then explain and model the next few steps by say-ing, "Remember how we regrouped in this one [pointing to model]. When we use pencil we regroup in a different way. We regroup by subtracting the one set of 3 that we already made. First we estimate the number of sets we can make here [pointing to 4] with this many in each set [pointing to 3]. It is one, so we write it here [write 1 in the quotient]. Next, we multiply the num-ber of sets by the number of items in each set [step 7]. Then we subtract the number of items in the set we made to see how many are left over [step 8]. We see that we cannot make any sets with 3 in a set, so we make the 10 into ten 1s and combine it with the five 1s to make fifteen 1s [step 9]. We can then make five sets with 3 in each set out of the fifteen 1s. Then we can multiply the number of sets by the number of items in each set to make 15 [step 10]. We can then subtract the number of items in the set we made to see how many items are left over [step 11]."

The solution process using the traditional symbolic form of division can be practiced by completing a number of items where a single-digit number (i.e., the divisor) is divided into a two-digit number (i.e., the dividend).

Make the transition from division of two-digit by single-digit numbers to problems that involve two digits divided by two digits and then to division of three digits by two –digits using sequences such as the following items, where each step resembles the one before it: $12\overline{)24}$, $12\overline{)25}$, $12\overline{)36}$, $12\overline{)39}$, $12\overline{)246}$, $12\overline{)264}$, $12\overline{)263}$, $12\overline{)240}$, and $12\overline{)204}$. The final item would resemble the following when solved by the students using manipultatives.

Step	
1	12$\overline{)204}$
2	#11$\overline{)\$\$1111}$
3	11111111111$\overline{)\$\$1111}$
4	11111111111$\overline{)\#1111}$

Step			
5		1	

11111111111$\overline{)\#\#\#\#\#\#\#\#\#\#\#\#\#\#\#\#\#\#1111}$

Step			
6		1	

11111111111$\overline{)\#\#\#\#\#\#\#\#\#\#\#111}$

1111111111
1111111111
1111111111
1111111111
1111111111
1111111111
1111111111
1111111111

Step			
7		1	7

11111111111$\overline{)\#\#\#\#\#\#\#\#\#\#\#111}$

1111111111
1111111111
1111111111
1111111111
1111111111
1111111111
1111111111
1111111111

Key: $ = 100's; # = 10's; and 1 = 1's

Students who accurately solve items equivalent to those listed above and who can represent them in a number of ways should be introduced to items that involve division of four digits by two digits similar to the following sequence: $12\overline{)2{,}448}$, $12\overline{)2{,}449}$, $12\overline{)2{,}648}$, $12\overline{)2{,}649}$, $12\overline{)2{,}460}$, $12\overline{)2{,}406}$, $12\overline{)4{,}206}$, $12\overline{)4{,}086}$, $12\overline{)4{,}008}$, and $12\overline{)4{,}009}$. At this point only two or three items should be included in a lesson and the students should be able to complete the items in their symbolic form quickly as the routine of the algorithm becomes more automatic.

The students should be able to complete the items with three-digit and four-digit dividends with manipulative and pictorial representations. This is an excellent time to introduce money and pose the problem, "If you had $264 and it was made of two $100s, six $10s and four $1s, how would you divide it evenly among 12 people?" or "How would you divide it to find out how much each person receives if there were 12 people involved."

Step	
1	$12\,people\overline{)\$264}$
2	$12\,/\$100, \$100 \quad \$10, \$10, \$10, \$10, \$10, \$10 \quad \$1, \$1, \$1, \$1$
3	$12\,/\$10, \$10, \$10, \$10, \$10, \$10 \qquad\qquad \$1, \$1, \$1, \$1$
	$\$10, \$10, \$10, \$10, \$10, \$10, \$10, \$10, \$10, \$10$
	$\$10, \$10, \$10, \$10, \$10, \$10, \$10, \$10\ \$10, \$10$
4	$\qquad\qquad\qquad\qquad\qquad 2$
	$12\,/\$10, \$10, \$10, \$10, \$10, \$10 \qquad\qquad \$1, \$1, \$1, \$1$
	$\$10, \$10, \$10, \$10, \$10, \$10, \$10, \$10, \$10, \$10$
	$\$10, \$10, \$10, \$10, \$10, \$10, \$10, \$10\ \$10, \$10$
5	$\qquad\qquad\qquad\qquad\qquad 2$
	$12\,/\$10, \$10, \$10, \$10, \$10, \$10 \qquad\qquad \$1, \$1, \$1, \$1$
	$\$10, \$10, \$10, \$10, \$10, \$10, \$10, \$10, \$10, \$10$
	$\$10, \$10, \$10, \$10, \$10, \$10, \$10, \$10$
	$\qquad\qquad\qquad\qquad\qquad \$1, \$1, \$1, \$1, \$1, \$1, \$1, \$1, \$1, \$1$
	$\qquad\qquad\qquad\qquad\qquad \$1, \$1, \$1, \$1, \$1, \$1, \$1, \$1, \$1, \$1$
6	$\qquad\qquad\qquad\qquad\qquad 2 \qquad\qquad\qquad\qquad 2$
	$12\,/\$10, \$10, \$10, \$10, \$10, \$10 \qquad\qquad \$1, \$1, \$1, \$1$
	$\$10, \$10, \$10, \$10, \$10, \$10, \$10, \$10, \$10, \$10$
	$\$10, \$10, \$10, \$10, \$10, \$10, \$10, \$10$
	$\qquad\qquad\qquad\qquad\qquad \$1, \$1, \$1, \$1, \$1, \$1, \$1, \$1\ \$1, \$1$
	$\qquad\qquad\qquad\qquad\qquad \$1, \$1, \$1, \$1, \$1, \$1, \$1, \$1, \$1, \$1$

A way to solve this problem using dollar bills as manipulatives is to convert the two $100s into $10s and compile a set of twenty-four $10s (step 3). The $10s could then be divided into two sets of twelve with two left over (step 4). The two extra $10 would then be converted to twenty $1s and combined with the four $1s that are already there (step 5). The twenty-four $1s are then grouped into two sets of twelve (step 6). Illustrations with money clearly show that we "don't move over because 12 does not go into 2." Instead it demonstrates that regrouping or renaming is the actual and accurate process. Students can work with many combinations of numbers using play money in denominations of $100s, $10s, and $1s with dollars and $1.00, $0.10, and $0.01 with dollars and cents.

Beyond combinations with two-digit divisors, we suggest that students estimate an answer and then use hand-held calculators for exact computations. Time that would have been spent doing computations with three or more digits can be devoted to problem solving.

Alternative Algorithms

The instructional approach to division described in the previous sections focuses mainly on the use of the traditional algorithm. The primary exception is the use of counting and the elimination of the need for multiplication and subtraction when dividing. Two additional algorithms can also be considered, and both approaches require students to be able to estimate. The first approach can be demonstrated with the problem $12\overline{)264}$ (step 1). First students have to estimate the number of 12s in 264. The students might say, "There are at least ten 12s in 264" (step 2). Because 144 12s remain, the students realize there are more 12s than they initially estimated and say "Let's try ten more" (step 3). And then realize that are "still two more sets of 12" (step 4). Finally the students will say "When we add them up we get twenty-two, so there are twenty-two sets of 12 in 264" (step 5). Or the students might begin with an estimate of 22 and say, "Twelve goes into 264 twenty-two times" (step 5).

2
$$10$$
$$12\overline{)264}$$

$$-\ 120$$

144

---

3   10
$$10$$
$$12\overline{)264}$$

$$-\ 120$$

144

$$-\ 120$$

24

---

4   2
10
$$10$$
$$12\overline{)264}$$

$$-\ 120$$

144

$$-\ 120$$

24

$$-\ 24$$

0

---

5   22
$$12\overline{)264}$$

The student might use a modified format as is shown in the process below, and complete the item by saying, "Twelve goes into 264 about ten times" [step 2]. The students can continue by saying, "Let's try twelve times" (step 3). Students can then complete the problem by saying "We can add them up and get twenty-two, so there are twenty-two sets of 12 in 264" (step 4)

Step		
1	12)264	
2	12)264	10
	− 120	
	144	
3	12)264	10
	− 120	
	144	12
	− 144	
	0	
4	12)264	10
	− 120	
	144	12
	− 144	
	0	$(10 + 12 = 22)$

## CHAPTER EIGHT

Hand-Held Calculators

The view of the authors is that hand-held calculators are an important and needed component of any program in arithmetic instruction and higher levels of mathematics. The place of the hand-held calculator must be strategically determined. The hand-held calculator should not be used to supplant, or take the place of, higher levels of knowing and doing. Accordingly, we recommend calculator use only after the students have demonstrated mastery of the meanings, principles, and procedures of single-digit and double-digit items and after the students have demonstrated a degree of competence and familiarity with items of greater complexity. In effect, the calculator should never be used to replace shortcomings with single-digit or double-digit items, although they can be used for drill and practice with those items. We collected a large amount of data (Cawley, Parmar, Yan, & Miller, 1996), focusing on one multiplication item: 496×348. The number of different student responses to this item was so great that any teacher confronted with such a variety of answers would find it impossible to correct every error made by the students. The use of the hand-held calculator would eliminate the great majority of these errors without clouding the performance qualities of the students.

Activity-Based Computer Participation

The great majority of computer-based activities in arithmetic involve the student as a passive participant in which one or more number combinations or word problems are displayed on the screen and the student types in a response, such as:

$$\begin{array}{r} 8 \\ +\,4 \\ \hline \end{array}$$

A boy has 3 dogs. A girl has 2 cats. Together, how many pets do the children have?

MYMATH (Cawley & Doan, 2002; Cawley & Foley, 2002) differs from most arithmetic software in that the student is an active participant who creates, edits, evaluates, or plays student-made files. The primary role of the teacher is to introduce the student to the computer and to demonstrate the procedures for the development of files. The screen displays options as shown below:

Program Options
Arithmetic Computation
Arithmetic Word Problems
Arithmetic Story Problems
Exit
Click on Choice

"Arithmetic Computation" is designed to enable the students to work with arithmetic computation items across the four operations of arithmetic; "Arithmetic Word Problems" enables the students to work with word problems of three to five sentences; and "Arithmetic Story Problems" enables the students to work with problems embedded in actual stories that are accompanied by questions. The latter provides for both quantitative reasoning and language/reading comprehension activities.

Assume the student selected "Arithmetic Computation" and the screen then shows:

Arithmetic Computation
Main Menu
Play
Create
Edit
Student Records
End Session
Click on Choice

"Create" involves the student in the creation of a file, in this instance to focus on arithmetic computation. The computation items can be of any type or form and for any level of appropriateness for the students. The files may be of any length, although they generally include about eight or more items. The student names the file and types in his/her initials and a first name. The date for the creation is designated, and if it is a teacher-created file, a password is required so as to deny student access until the teacher allows, as in a test setting.

Arithmetic Computation

Create

Type in name of file:	ROSE
Type in your initials:	A
Type in your first name:	ALICIA
Type in date:	4/3/2006
Enter Password:	(Required only for Teacher)
Is it correct (Y/N)?	

"Play" has the student or others activate a given file and complete a selected number of items within the file. The file may contain more items than the student desires to do. Therefore, the student may select a given number. For example, on this day the file contains twenty-four items and the student desires to only do six of them. The student selects "6" and six items are selected at random. Assume this same student reactivated the file and wished to do six more items. Six items are selected at random and the student may or may not encounter any of the items from a previous play activity as illustrated below.

Arithmetic Computation

Selected file name: ROSE created by ALICIA_A.		
Total number of items: 2	Record # 1	
How many items do you want to do?	2	Press Enter
Now play item	1	

$$\begin{array}{r} 3 \\ + 5 \\ \hline 8 \end{array}$$

The program also maintains a complete record of student performance. This includes date, correct or incorrect for each item, time for completion of each item, total number of items correct for the session and total time for the session. Should the teacher desire to create a file and utilize this as a test, the program requires a password so that students may not change or vary items. The data collected for the teacher will be the same as that for the students and may be as extensive as the school year. The "Student Record Reports" have two components as shown below.

Student Records Report
Progress Report
Student Responses
Main Menu

Within the "Student Records Report" the student(s) or teacher will find detailed information on student performance.

Arithmetic Computation

Student Records Manager

Select author:	ALICIA_A has 1 file.
ALICIA_A	*Progress Report*
	Player Responses
	Delete Player Record
	Main Menu

The "Progress Report" lists all students who have used a file. The "Player Response" provides detailed information on all students who have used a file.

Progress Report: Word Problems

Author: Bob S

Record #	Player Name	File Name	Edit #	Date	Number of Items	Percent Correct	Time of Session
2	Alicia	Book	1	2/4/06	2	100%	16
1	Ben B	Book	1	2/8/06	12	50%	137

"Edit" provides an opportunity for the student to reenter a given file and make additions, corrections, or amendments to the file. MYMATH does not provide the correct responses. These must be entered by the student when the items are created. Occasionally, a student may enter an incorrect response when creating a file. Another student may play the file, provide a correct response and be told that it is incorrect. This is intentional as a major element of MYMATH is student engagement and interaction. The students are encouraged to discuss the item and, if necessary, seek the assistance of the teacher to agree upon a correct response. The student who created the file, may then turn to the edit component and enter the correct response.

Player Responses Report—Story Problems

Author of Problems: Bob_B		
Player Name: BEN_B	Record ID#: 1	Date of Use: 02-20-06
File Name:	BOOK	
Number of Items Attempted:	2	
Percent Correct:	2	
Total Time for Session		
Item #1	Donna has 6 books. She has 2 more than her sister. How many books does her sister have?	
Answer:	4	
Player Response:	8	
Correct/Incorrect:	Incorrect	
Time for Item:	7	
Item # 2	Donna has 6 books. She has 2 more books than her sister. How many books do the have together?	
Answer:	10	
Player Response:	8	
Correct/Incorrect:	Incorrect	
Time for Item:	40	

Note that the information set or stem is the same for both problems. In this instance, the questions vary the problem type.

Note also that there is a complete record of the responses of the student and this record is maintained throughout the year for each and every student.

Arithmetic Computation

Edit

Select file to be edited	
ROSE	*Display/Print Item*
	Change Item
	Delete Item
	Add Item
	End Session
Selected file: None	
Total number of items: 0	

Evaluation

While percent correct and speed of completion are important, of greater importance is the performance of the student across the number of files created for the year. This will include the number of different files, the number of edits on a file, the number of different students who played a file or files and an examination of the types of items within a file. For example, with word problem files, did the student create a variety of different problems? With respect to student performance in terms of speed and accuracy, this can be determined by the teacher, who can create as many different files as desired.

Activities involving the arithmetic operations and counting should be based on meaning-ful instances of application and problem solving. The rationale for learning calculation should be established by using calculation to solve meaningful and real-life problems and in solving problems related to other subject matter. The use of computational activities to solve long-term problems should be integral to school-initiated problems. Recording weather and temperature, calculating data on school events, and other long-term activities should be natural activities throughout the school. In fact, it seems highly desirable to consider the replacement of drill and practice worksheets with meaningful data collection and analyses such that students would actu-ally do more calculations, have more practice, and produce more solutions to problems.

## CHAPTER NINE

Concluding Comments

Activities involving the arithmetic operations and counting should be based on meaningful instances of application and problem solving. The rationale for learning calculations should be established by using calculation to solve meaningful and real-life problems and in solving problems related to other subject matter. The use of computational activities to solve long-term problems should be integral to school initiated problems. Recording weather and temperature, calculating data on school events, and other long-term activities should be natural activities throughout the school. In fact, it seems highly desirable to consider the replacement of drill and practice worksheets with meaningful data collection and analyses such that students would actually do more calculations, have more practice, and produce more solutions to problems.

Computational Sequences

Addition

	Examples		Descriptor
A1	**6 + 3**	**4 + 2**	**One Digit + One Digit; No Renaming**
A2	9 + 7	8 + 4	One Digit + One Digit; Renaming 1s
A3	6 + 2 + 1	3 + 5 + 1	One Digit + One Digit + One Digit; No Renaming
A4	4 + 8 + 3	3 + 9 + 5	One Digit + One Digit + One Digit; Renaming 1s
A5	**36 + 3**	**63 + 4**	**Two Digit + One Digit; No Renaming**
A6	58 + 9	47 + 8	Two Digit + One Digit; Renaming 1s
A7	98 + 8	94 + 9	Two Digit + One Digit; Renaming 1s and 10s
A8	53 + 32	35 + 52	Two Digit + Two Digit; No Renaming
A9	65 + 19	74 + 18	Two Digit + Two Digit; Renaming 1s
A10	77 + 51	83 + 64	Two Digit + Two Digit; Renaming 10s
A11	**79 + 57**	**65 + 68**	**Two Digit + Two Digit; Renaming 1s and 10s**
A12	6 + 2 + 9	7 + 8 +3	One Digit + One Digit + One Digit; Renaming 1s
A13	**41 + 3 + 2**	**64 + 2 + 3**	**Two Digit + One Digit + One Digit; No Renaming**
A14	65 + 8 + 9	38 + 9 + 5	Two Digit + One Digit + One Digit; Renaming 1s
A15	**94 + 9 + 8**	**97 + 7 + 9**	**Two Digit + One Digit + One Digit; Renaming 1s and 10s**
A16	63 + 24 + 2	34 + 22 + 1	Two Digit + Two Digit + One Digit; No Renaming
A17	39 + 24 + 3	64 + 5 + 16	Two Digit + Two Digit + One Digit; Renaming 1s
A18	54 + 59 + 8	73 + 9 + 56	Two Digit + Two Digit + One Digit; Renaming 1s and 10s
A19	31 + 12 + 15	23 + 41 + 32	Two Digit + Two Digit + Two Digit; No Renaming
A20	38 + 24 + 34	65 + 16 + 17	Two Digit + Two Digit + Two Digit; Renaming 1s
A21	42 + 30 + 83	31 + 51 + 76	Two Digit + Two Digit + Two Digit; Renaming 10s
A22	**58 + 97 + 48**	**29 + 62 + 51**	**Two Digit + Two Digit + Two Digit, Renaming 1s and 10s**
A23	341 + 5	243 + 6	Three Digit + One Digit; No Renaming
A24	541 + 42	336 + 61	Three Digit + Two Digit; No Renaming
A25	234 + 345	513 + 283	Three Digit + Three Digit; No Renaming
A26	234 + 8	317 + 5	Three Digit + One Digit; Renaming 1s
A27	348 + 71	785 + 84	Three Digit + Two Digit; Renaming 10s
A28	458 + 87	379 + 93	Three Digit + Two Digit; Renaming 1s and 10s
A29	247 + 138	319 + 257	Three Digit + Three Digit; Renaming 1s
A30	264 + 172	281 + 253	Three Digit + Three Digit; Renaming 10s
A31	633 + 714	814 + 825	Three Digit + Three Digit; Renaming 100s
A32	365 + 475	489 + 295	Three Digit + Three Digit; Renaming 1s and 10s
A33	538 + 719	719 + 436	Three Digit + Three Digit; Renaming 1s and 100s
A34	682 + 555	971 + 371	Three Digit + Three Digit; Renaming 10s and 100s
A35	586 + 875	779 + 358	Three Digit + Three Digit; Renaming 1s, 10s, and 100s

Addition

	Examples		Descriptor
A36	**324 + 22 + 1**	**421 + 45 + 3**	**Three Digit + Two Digit + One Digit; No Renaming**
A37	438 + 34 + 8	246 + 7 + 34	Three Digit + Two Digit + One Digit; Renaming 1s
A38	734 + 6 + 87	8 + 44 + 393	Three Digit + Two Digit + One Digit; Renaming 1s and 10s
A39	**645 + 47 + 94**	**448 + 78 + 98**	**Three Digit + Two Digit + Two Digit; Renaming 1s and 10s**
A40	**234 + 132 + 12**	**633 + 12 + 242**	**Three Digit + Three Digit + Two Digit; No Renaming**
A41	526 + 29 + 334	634 + 235 + 17	Three Digit + Three Digit + Two Digit; Renaming 1s
A42	471 + 36 + 357	174 + 276 + 87	Three Digit + Three Digit + Two Digit; Renaming 1s and 10s
A43	**862 + 74 + 653**	**234 + 72 + 953**	**Three Digit + Three Digit + Two Digit; Renaming 10s and 100s**
A44	616 + 52 + 718	26 + 843 + 623	Three Digit + Three Digit + Two Digit; Renaming 1s and 100s
A45	674 + 29 + 835	876 + 585 + 12	Three Digit + Three Digit + Two Digit; Renaming 1s, 10s, and 100s
A46	940 + 864 + 58	806 + 87 + 753	Three Digit + Three Digit + Two Digit; Zeros; Renaming 1s, 10s, and 100s
A47	**234 + 541 + 223**	**423 + 154 + 322**	**Three Digit + Three Digit + Three Digit; No Renaming**
A48	354 + 217 + 126	432 + 124 + 214	Three Digit + Three Digit + Three Digit; Renaming 1s
A49	**354 + 276 + 135**	**244 + 378 + 253**	**Three Digit + Three Digit + Three Digit; Renaming 1s and 10s**
A50	568 + 271 + 428	633 + 729 + 486	Three Digit + Three Digit + Three Digit; Renaming 1s, 10s, and 100s
A51	783 + 309 + 480	508 + 493 + 470	Three Digit + Three Digit + Three Digit; Renaming 1s, 10s, and 100s, Zeros
A52	3762 + 2135	4351 + 4348	Four Digit + Four Digit; No Renaming
A53	6732 + 2149	4573 + 3219	Four Digit + Four Digit; Renaming 1s
A54	5477 + 3167	3167 + 4376	Four Digit + Four Digit; Renaming 1s and 10s
A55	3486 + 2765	4796 + 2569	Four Digit + Four Digit; Renaming 1s, 10s, and 100s
A56	5894 + 6588	7539 + 5674	Four Digit + Four Digit; Renaming 1s, 10s, 100s, and 1000s
A57	**8560 + 4574**	**3820 + 8593**	**Four Digit + Four Digit; Renaming 10s, 100s, and 1000s, Zero 1s**
A58	5609 + 6895	5906 + 8598	Four Digit + Four Digit; Renaming 1s, 10s, 100s, and 1000s, Zero 10s
A59	**6050 + 4678**	**7050 + 5294**	**Four Digit + Four Digit; Renaming 10s and 1000s, Zero 1s and 100s**
A60	3006 + 7438	5009 + 8129	Four Digit + Four Digit; Renaming 1s and 1000s; Zero 10s and 100s
A61	4006 + 7397	3008 + 8795	Four Digit + Four Digit; Renaming 1s, 10s, and 1000s; Zero 10s and 100s
A62	**5009 + 8997**	**6009 + 8996**	**Four Digit + Four Digit; Renaming 1s, 10s, 100s, and 1000s; Zero 10s and 100s**
A63	3624 + 2153 + 2122	4213 + 4325 + 1451	Four Digit + Four Digit + Four Digit; No Renaming
A64	6425 + 2146 + 1225	2358 + 3425 + 1116	Four Digit + Four Digit + Four Digit; Renaming 1s
A65	6452 + 1242 + 2163	5382 + 1392 + 2174	Four Digit + Four Digit + Four Digit; Renaming 10s
A66	3421 + 2723 + 1632	6421 + 1941 + 2521	Four Digit + Four Digit + Four Digit; Renaming 100s
A67	5432 + 6213 + 4134	6313 + 9341 + 4231	Four Digit + Four Digit + Four Digit; Renaming 1000s
A68	2157 + 2188 + 2157	3358 + 1343 + 2135	Four Digit + Four Digit + Four Digit; Renaming 1s and 10s
A69	4423 + 2615 + 1537	1527 + 2537 + 2816	Four Digit + Four Digit + Four Digit; Renaming 1s and 100s
A70	2432 + 2542 + 2773	1752 + 2751 + 2881	Four Digit + Four Digit + Four Digit; Renaming 10s and 100s
A71	6251 + 6152 + 7253	3172 + 6273 + 4431	Four Digit + Four Digit + Four Digit; Renaming 10s and 1000s
A72	6555 + 1345 + 1465	2674 + 2543 + 3574	Four Digit + Four Digit + Four Digit; Renaming 1s, 10s, and 100s
A73	7466 + 4637 + 3663	3887 + 8425 + 7654	Four Digit + Four Digit + Four Digit; Renaming 1s, 10s, 100s, and 1000s
A74	3820 + 6507 + 6074	7650 + 5709 + 5077	Four Digit + Four Digit + Four Digit; Renaming 1s, 10s, 100s, and 1000s; Zeros scrambled

Subtraction

	Examples		Descriptor
S1	5 − 4	6 − 3	One Digit − One Digit
S2	**26 − 3**	**38 − 2**	**Two Digit − One Digit; No Renaming**
S3	28 − 15	45 − 32	Two Digit − Two Digit; No Renaming
S4	**24 − 6**	**32 − 4**	**Two Digit − One Digit; Renaming 1s**
S5	**54 − 26**	**83 − 27**	**Two Digit − Two Digit; Renaming 1s**
S6	565 − 2	867 − 5	Three Digit − One Digit; No Renaming
S7	857 − 24	975 − 43	Three Digit − Two Digit; No Renaming
S8	**471 − 4**	**492 − 3**	**Three Digit − One Digit; Renaming 1s**
S9	763 − 38	872 − 44	Three Digit − Two Digit; Renaming 1s
S10	365 − 63	828 − 54	Three Digit − Two Digit; Renaming 10s
S11	632 − 27	826 − 58	Three Digit − Two Digit; Renaming 1s and 10s
S12	**612 − 28**	**613 − 47**	**Three Digit − Two Digit; Renaming 1s and 10s; Zero 10s**
S13	50 − 8	30 − 5	Two Digit − One Digit; Renaming 1s; Zero 1s
S14	**40 − 18**	**60 − 27**	**Two Digit − Two Digit; Renaming 1s; Zero 1s**
S15	**365 − 7**	**444 − 9**	**Three Digit − One Digit; Renaming 1s**
S16	780 − 33	350 − 17	Three Digit − Two Digit; Renaming 1s; Zero 1s
S17	540 − 67	270 − 91	Three Digit − Two Digit; Renaming 1s and 10s; Zero 1s
S18	**207 − 54**	**806 − 21**	**Three Digit − Two Digit; Renaming 10s; Zero 10s**
S19	605 − 77	405 − 86	Three Digit − Two Digit; Renaming 1s and 10s; Zero 10s
S20	600 − 40	700 − 30	Three Digit − Two Digit; Renaming 10s; Zero 1s and 10s
S21	**700 − 53**	**600 − 12**	**Three Digit − Two Digit; Renaming 1s and 10s; Zero 1s and 10s**
S22	**546 − 321**	**638 − 417**	**Three Digit − Three Digit; No Renaming**
S23	371 − 218	465 − 347	Three Digit − Three Digit; Renaming 1s
S24	527 − 245	649 − 489	Three Digit − Three Digit; Renaming 10s
S25	724 − 468	733 − 648	Three Digit − Three Digit; Renaming 1s and 10s
S26	650 − 443	870 − 542	Three Digit − Three Digit; Renaming 1s; Zeros 1s
S27	**507 − 236**	**608 − 314**	**Three Digit − Three Digit; Renaming 10s; Zero 10s**
S28	340 − 156	850 − 274	Three Digit − Three Digit; Renaming 1s and 10s; Zero 1s
S29	405 − 256	704 − 387	Three Digit − Three Digit; Renaming 1s and 10s; Zero 10s
S30	600 − 238	800 − 384	Three Digit − Three Digit; Renaming 1s and 10s; Zero 1s and 10s
S31	8653 − 3621	4947 − 1335	Four Digit − Four Digit; No Renaming
S32	7652 − 2357	3983 − 1256	Four Digit − Four Digit; Renaming 1s
S33	**8545 − 2172**	**5448 − 3166**	**Four Digit − Four Digit; Renaming 10s**
S34	8378 − 1831	9426 − 5614	Four Digit − Four Digit; Renaming 100s
S35	**5232 − 1754**	**7322 − 5478**	**Four Digit − Four Digit; Renaming 100s, 10s, and 1s**
S36	8560 − 4537	7770 − 1338	Four Digit − Four Digit; Renaming 1s; Zero 1s
S37	6800 − 2663	5900 − 3129	Four Digit − Four Digit; Renaming 1s and 10s; Zero 1s and 10s
S38	4080 − 1662	7070 − 1838	Four Digit − Four Digit; Renaming 1s and 100s; Zero 1s and 100s
S39	9005 − 1262	7004 − 4652	Four Digit − Four Digit; Renaming 10s and 100s; Zero 10s and 100s
S40	5007 − 2339	6004 − 3278	Four Digit − Four Digit; Renaming 1s, 10s, and 100s; Zero 10s and 100s
S41	**8000 − 6345**	**7000 − 2972**	**Four Digit − Four Digit; Renaming 1s, 10s, and 100s; Zero 1s, 10s, and 100s**

Multiplication

	Examples		Descriptor
M1	2 × 2	2 × 3	One Digit × One Digit; No Renaming
M2	6 × 4	5 × 3	One Digit × One Digit; Renaming
M3	23 × 2	43 × 2	Two Digit × One Digit; No Renaming
M4	**25 × 3**	**17 × 2**	**Two Digit × One Digit; Renaming 1s**
M5	43 × 12	32 × 21	Two Digit × Two Digit; No Renaming

Multiplication

	Examples		Descriptor
M6	26 × 13	17 × 14	Two Digit × Two Digit; Renaming 1s
M7	**48 × 14**	**27 × 16**	**Two Digit × Two Digit; Renaming 1s and 10s**
M8	53 × 64	74 × 75	Two Digit × Two Digit; Renaming all
M9	60 × 45	40 × 76	Two Digit × Two Digit; Renaming 10s; Zero 1s
M10	**36 × 40**	**74 × 60**	**Two Digit × Two Digit; Renaming 1s and 10s**
M11	243 × 2	321 × 3	Tree Digit × One Digit; No Renaming
M12	**863 × 8**	**389 × 7**	**Three Digit × One Digit; Renaming 1s, 10s, and 100s**
M13	340 × 8	560 × 3	Three Digit × One Digit; Renaming 10s and 100s; Zero 1s
M14	305 × 6	708 × 3	Three Digit × One Digit; Renaming 1s and 100s; Zero 10s
M15	121 × 13	132 × 21	Three Digit × Two Digit; No Renaming
M16	316 × 13	328 × 12	Three Digit × Two Digit; Renaming 1s
M17	263 × 23	372 × 12	Three Digit × Two Digit; Renaming 10s
M18	423 × 13	513 × 13	Three Digit × Two Digit; Renaming 100s
M19	**567 × 38**	**793 × 64**	**Three Digit × Two Digit; Renaming all**
M20	310 × 12	220 × 23	Three Digit × Two Digit; No Renaming; Zero 1s
M21	202 × 21	301 × 23	Three Digit × Two Digit; No Renaming; Zero 10s
M22	750 × 29	660 × 84	Three Digit × Two Digit; Renaming 10s and 100s; Zero 1s
M23	407 × 45	507 × 37	Three Digit × Two Digit; Renaming 1s and 100s; Zero 10s
M24	234 × 122	213 × 322	Three Digit × Three Digit; No Renaming
M25	**496 × 843**	**585 × 376**	**Three Digit × Three Digit; Renaming all**
M26	430 × 576	560 × 897	Three Digit × Three Digit; Renaming 10s and 100s; Zero 1s
M27	706 × 576	803 × 444	Three Digit × Three Digit; Renaming 1s and 100s; Zero 10s
M28	**600 × 436**	**700 × 883**	**Three Digit × Three Digit; Renaming 100s; Zero 1s and 10s**
M29	708 × 600	603 × 400	Three Digit × Three Digit; Renaming scrambled; Zero scrambled
M30	**5030 × 4200**	**2050 × 2300**	**Four Digit × Four Digit; Renaming scrambled; Zero scrambled; This item is a cross-check for zero use**

Division

	Examples		Descriptor
D1	3)9	2)8	One Digit ÷ One Digit; No Renaming; No remainder
D2	3)7	4)6	One Digit ÷ One Digit; No Renaming; Remainder
D3	**2)14**	**5)15**	**Two Digit ÷ One Digit; Renaming 10s; No remainder**
D4	**3)26**	**5)12**	**Two Digit ÷ One Digit; Renaming 10s; Remainder**
D5	**3)936**	**4)448**	**Three Digit ÷ One Digit; No Renaming; No remainder**
D6	4)164	3)246	Three Digit ÷ One Digit; Renaming 100s; No remainder
D7	**5)163**	**5)333**	**Three Digit ÷ One Digit; Renaming 100s and 10s; Remainder**
D8	4)480	3)360	Three Digit ÷ One Digit; No Renaming; No remainder; Zero 1s
D9	3)906	4)808	Tree Digit ÷ One Digit; No Renaming; No remainder; Zero 10s
D10	**7)504**	**6)204**	**Three Digit ÷ One Digit; Renaming 100s and 10s; Zero 10s**
D11	5)200	8)400	Three Digit ÷ One Digit; Renaming 100s; Zero 10s and 1s
D12	**12)48**	**14)42**	**Two Digit ÷ Two Digit; Renaming 10s; No remainder**

Division

Examples		Descriptor
D13	16)51 12)38	Two Digit ÷ Two Digit; Renaming 10s; Remainder
D14	16)486 22)449	Three Digit ÷ Two Digit; Renaming 100s; Remainder
D15	**26)734 14)472**	**Three Digit ÷ Two Digit; Renaming 100s and 10s; No remainder**
D16	16)851 28)369	Three Digit ÷ Two Digit; Renaming 100s and 10s; Remainder
D17	14)390 43)380	Three Digit ÷ Two Digit; Renaming 100s and 10s; Remainder; Zero 1s
D18	**12)207 15)405**	**Three Digit ÷ Two Digit; Renaming 100s and 10s; Remainder; Zero 10s**
D19	**15)600 20)600**	**Three Digit ÷ Two Digit; Renaming 100s; No remainder; Zero 100s and 10s**
D20	12)4956 23)4945	Four Digit ÷ Two Digit; Renaming 1000s and 100s; No remainder
D21	28)2457 16)1457	Four Digit ÷ Two Digit; Renaming 1000s and 100s; Remainder
D22	28)2650 53)2140	Four Digit ÷ Two Digit; Renaming 1000s and 100s; Remainder; Zero 1s
D23	**26)4060 31)2090**	**Four Digit ÷ Two Digit; Renaming 1000s and 100s; Remainder; Zero 100s and 1s**
D24	57)3009 34)1006	Four Digit ÷ Two Digit; Renaming 1000s and 100s; Remainder; Zero 100s and 10s
D25	22)2000 43)3000	Four Digit ÷ Two Digit; Renaming 1000s and 100s; Remainder; Zero 100s, 10s, and 1s
D26	231)6468 213)4473	Four Digit ÷ Three Digit; Renaming 1000s and 100s; No remainder
D27	**126)5167 218)2618**	**Four Digit ÷ Three Digit; Renaming 1000s and 100s; Remainder**
D28	213)6730 412)5340	Four Digit ÷ Three Digit; Renaming 1000s and 100s; Remainder; Zero 1s
D29	322)7400 214)4900	Four Digit ÷ Three Digit; Renaming 1000s and 100s; Remainder; Zero 10s and 1s
D30	**148)3008 438)6004**	**Four Digit ÷ Three Digit; Renaming 1000s and 100s; Remainder; Zero 100s and 10s**

References

Ashlock, R. (1976). *Error patterns in computation: A semi-programmed approach.* Columbus, OH: Charles E. Merrill Co.

Baroody, A. J. (1990). How and when should place-value concepts and skills be taught? *Journal for Research in Mathematics, 21*(4), 281–86.

Bruner, J. (1966). *Toward a theory of instruction.* Cambridge, MA: Harvard University Press.

Bryant, D. P., Bryant, B. R., & Hammill, D. D. (2000). Characteristic behaviors of students with LD who have teacher-identified math weaknesses. *Journal of Learning Disabilities, 33,* 168–77, 199.

Burnham, C. G. (1849). *A new system of arithmetic, on an improved plan.* New York: D. Appleton & Company.

Carroll, W., & Porter, D. (1998). Alternative algorithms for whole-number operations. In L. J. Morrow (Ed.), *The teaching and learning of algorithms in school mathematics* (pp. 106–14). Reston, VA: National Council of Teachers of Mathematics.

Cawley, J. F., & Doan, T. (2002). MYMATH: A student-driven program. Storrs, CT.

Cawley, J., Fitzmaurice, A. M., Goodstein, H., Lepore, A., Sedlak, R., & Althaus, V. (1974). *Project MATH.* Tulsa, OK: Educational Progress Corporation.

Cawley, J. F., & Foley, T. E. (2002). Connecting math and science for all students. *Teaching Exceptional Children, 34*(4), 14–19.

Cawley, J. F., & Goodman, J. O. (1969). Arithmetic problem solving: A demonstration with the mentally handicapped. *Exceptional Children, 36*(2), 83–88.

Cawley, J. F., Parmar, R. S., Lucas-Fusco, L. M., Kilian, J. D., & Foley, T. E. (2007). Place value and mathematics for students with mild disabilities: Data and suggested practices. *Learning Disabilities: A Contemporary Journal, 5*(1), 21–39.

Cawley, J. F., Parmar, R. S., Yan, W. F., & Miller, J. (1996). Arithmetic computation abilities of students with learning disabilities: Implications for instruction. *Learning Disabilities Research & Practice, 11*(4), 230–37.

Cawley, J. F., & Reines, R. (1996). Mathematics as communication: Using the interactive unit. *Teaching Exceptional Children, 28*(2), 29–34.

Cawley, J., Parmar, R., Foley, T. E., Salmon, S., & Roy, S. (2001). Arithmetic performance of students with mild disabilities and general education students on selected arithmetic tasks: Implications for standards and programming. *Exceptional Children, 67*(3), 311–28.

CEC (Council for Exceptional Children). (1998). *What Every Special Educator Should Know,* 3rd ed. Reston, VA: Author

Encyclopedia Britannica. (2003). *Math in context: Going the distance.* Austin, TX: Holt, Rinehart, & Winston.

Federal Register. (1999). Rules and Regulations to P.L. 105-17.

Foley, T. E., Parmar, R., Cawley, J. F. (2003). Expanding the agenda in mathematics problem solving for students with mild disabilities: Suggestions for method and content. *Learning Disabilities: A Multidisciplinary Journal, 12*(3), 113–24.

Foley, T. E., Parmar, R., & Cawley, J. F. (2004). Expanding the agenda in mathematics problem solving for students with mild disabilities: Alternate representations. *Learning Disabilities: A Multidisciplinary Journal, 13*(1), 7–16.

Fuchs, L. S., & Fuchs, D. (2002). Mathematical problem-solving profiles of students with mathematics disabilities with and without comorbid reading disabilities. *Journal of Learning Disabilities, 35*(6), 563–73.

Fuson, K. (1990). Issues in place-value and multidigit addition and subtraction learning and teaching. *Journal for Research in Mathematics Education, 21*(4), 274–80.

Gavin, M. K., Findell, C., Greenes, C., & Sheffield, L. (2000). *Awesome math problems for creative thinking.* Chicago, IL: Creative Publications.

Gersten, R., & Chard, D. (1999). Number sense: Rethinking arithmetic instruction for students with mathematical disabilities. *The Journal of Special Education, 33*, 18–28.

Ginsburg, H. (1989). *Children arithmetic: How they learn it and how to teach it,* 2nd ed. Austin, TX: Pro-Ed.

Glover, M. (1993). *The effect of the hand-held calculator on the computation and problem-solving achievement of students with learning disabilities.* Unpublished doctoral dissertation, State University of New York at Buffalo.

Harding, D., Gust, A., Goldhawk, S., & Bierman, M. (1993). The effects of the interactive unit on the computational skills of students with learning disabilities and students with mild cognitive impairments. *Learning Disabilities: A Multidiscipline Journal, 4*, 53–65.

House, P., & Coxford, A. (1995). *Connecting mathematics across the curriculum.* Reston, VA: National Council of Teachers of Mathematics.

Kamii, C., & Dominick, A. (1998). The harmful effects of algorithms in grades 1–4. In L. J. Morrow (Ed.), *The teaching and learning of algorithms in school mathematics* (pp. 36–140). Reston, VA: National Council of Teachers of Mathematics.

Kamii, C., Lewis, B., & Livingston, C. (1993). Primary arithmetic: Children inventing their own procedures. *Arithmetic Teacher, 41*(4), 200–203.

Kleinert, H., Green, P., Hurte, M., Clayton, J., & Oetinger, C. (2002). Creating and using meaningful alternative assessments. *Teaching Exceptional Children, 34*, 40–47.

Lee, K. S. (1991). Left-to-right computations and estimation. *School Science and Mathematics, 91*(5), 199–201.

Miller, S., & Mercer, C. (1993). Using data to learn concrete-semiconcrete-abstract instruction for students with math disabilities. *Learning Disabilities Research and Practice, 8*, 89–96.

Morrow, L. J. (Ed.). (1998). *The teaching and learning of algorithms in school mathematics.* Reston, VA: National Council of Teachers of Mathematics.

Muma, J. R. (1978). *Language handbook: Concepts, assessment, intervention.* Englewood Cliffs, NJ: Prentice-Hall, Inc.

NCTM (National Council of Teachers of Mathematics). (2000). *Principles and standards for school mathematics.* Reston, VA: Author.

Neufeldt, V., & Sparks, A. (1990). *Webster's new world dictionary.* New York, NY: Warner Books, Inc.

Parmar, R., & Cawley, J. (1995). Mathematics curricula frameworks: Goals for general and special education. *Focus on Learning Problems in Mathematics, 17*(2), 50–66.

Peterson, S. K., Mercer, C. D., & O'Shea, L. (1988). Teaching learning disabled students place value using the concrete to abstract sequence. *Learning Disabilities Research, 4*(1), 52–56.

Philipp, R. A. (1996). Multicultural mathematics and alternative algorithms. *Teaching Children Mathematics, 3*(3), 128–33.

Polya, G. (1962). *Mathematical discovery: On understanding, learning, and teaching problem solving,* volume 2. New York: Wiley.

Putnam, R. T., DeBettencourt, L. U., & Leinhardt, D. (1990). Understanding the derived-fact strategies in addition and subtraction. *Cognition and Instruction, 7,* 245–85.

Reimer, L., & Reimer, W. (1995). Connecting mathematics with its history: Powerful rational linkage. In P. Hose & A. Coxford (Eds.), *Connecting mathematics across the curriculum* (pp. 104–114). Reston, VA: National Council of Teachers of Mathematics.

Reisman, F. K. (1977). *Diagnostic teaching of elementary school mathematics: Methods and content.* Chicago, IL: Rand McNally College Publishing Co.

Riley, M., & Greeno, J. (1988). Developmental analysis of understanding language about quantities and of solving problems. *Cognition and Instruction, 5,* 49–101.

Rose, B. (1989). Writing and mathematics: Theory and practice. In P. Connolly & T. Vilardi (Eds.), *Writing to learn mathematics and science* (pp. 15–30). New York: Teachers College Press.

Seguin, E. (1866). *Idiocy and its treatment by the physiological method.* New York: William Wood.

Wiig, E., & Semel, E. (1976). *Language disabilities in children and adolescents.* Columbus, OH: Charles E. Merrill Publishing Company.

About the Authors

JOHN CAWLEY is a special educator whose fifty-three years of work has focused on curriculum, instruction, and assessment as they relate to programs for students with disabilities. His educational background consists of a bachelor's degree from the University of Rhode Island and an MA and PhD from the University of Connecticut. He is professor emeritus from the University of Connecticut in 1979 and professor emeritus from the State University of New York at Buffalo in 1998. Dr. Cawley is currently an educational consultant.

ANNE FITZMAURICE HAYES, dean emerita of the University of Hartford, spent her professional life in higher education, focusing on instruction and assessment in mathematics, especially for those students finding mathematics especially challenging. Dr. Fitzmaurice earned her MA in teaching at Saint Joseph College in West Hartford, Connecticut, and her PhD from the University of Connecticut.

TERESA E. FOLEY is an instructor of mathematics at Asnuntuck Community College in Enfield, Connecticut. Her professional interests are in assessment and effective instruction in mathematics with students of all ages who experience difficulty learning mathematics. Dr. Foley earned her bachelor's degree in finance from the University of Connecticut, her master's of education degree in curriculum and instruction from Ohio University, and her PhD in special education from the University of Connecticut.